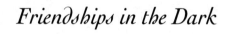

Friendships in the Dark

Friendships in the Dark

A Blind Woman's Story
of the People and Pets
Who Light Up Her World

Phyllis Campbell

B
Brett Books, Inc.
Brooklyn, New York

Published in the United States of America by Brett Books, Inc., P.O. Box 290-637, Brooklyn, New York 11229-0011.

Library of Congress Cataloging-in-Publication Data

Campbell, Phyllis, date
    Friendships in the dark : a blind woman's story of the people and
    pets who light up her world / Phyllis Campbell.—1st ed.
        p.   cm.
    ISBN 0-9636620-4-X
    1. Campbell, Phyllis, date.   2. Blind women—United States—
Biography.   3. Pets   I. Title.
HV1792.C35A3   1996
362.4'1'092—dc20
[B]   96-2412

First Edition
Manufactured in the United States of America
Printed on acid-free paper
96 97 98 99 00 10 9 8 7 6 5 4 3 2 1

Book design by C. Linda Dingler

For my friend Helen McGee,
my brother, Lively,
and all the others who walk with me in memory.

I will bring the blind by a way which they know not; in paths which they know not will I lead them; I will make darkness light before them, and crooked places straight. These things will I do, and I will not forsake them.

ISAIAH 42:16

Contents

CONTENTS

Friendships in the Dark

Prologue

Everything has its wonders, even darkness and silence, and I learn, whatever state I am in, therein to be content.

HELEN KELLER

The wind rose in the night, sending the last of the leaves flying from the trees in a glorious mad dance before their final sleep. Early this morning I saw them there where they lay on the lawn, dark and almost shapeless, giving themselves back to the earth that had nourished them. Above my head, the bare branches whispered of winter and the coming of yet another spring.

There is nothing in this description to indicate that it was written by a person who is blind, but it was. Since birth I have been totally blind. Yet I have never felt cheated of the rich beauty the world has to give. For as long as I can remember I have reached out to the world around me, giving and taking all the good things life has to offer.

For me and others who are born blind, the world with its

beauty, or its ugliness, is sometimes more real than it is for those who depend on physical sight. We touch, we hear, we smell, we taste, and we feel—we use all our senses except for sight, and then the image is ours.

Contrary to popular belief, we, the blind, do not possess special powers that enable us to hear more or to know more than our sighted peers. These so-called compensations come through the painstaking development of our remaining senses. My sense of hearing, for instance, is probably no better than that of most sighted people of my age, yet I invariably hear more than they do. This isn't the result of some mysterious ability of mine. I have learned over the years to listen and to interpret what I hear.

Often people are confused when the blind talk about seeing. Why would we say such a thing? The answer is simple. Since we live in a world inhabited predominantly by those who see with their physical eyes, it would be ridiculous, as well as embarrassing for everyone, to use expressions that are different from those used by others. I do see, even if it is with my fingers, and my nose, and my ears. And my world is filled with the same marvelous colors as everyone else's—it's just that I view them from a different perspective.

Of course, I didn't actually "see" the leaves on my lawn or the bare branches blowing overhead, but I knew they were there. My fingertips explored the pathetic things, which so recently had been filled with the beauty of their shape and texture. Surely, such pitiful things must be dark! As I listened, the branches gave off a dry, sad sound as they moved in the wind, and I knew they were bare.

A squirrel chattered a warning to me and leaped to the metal roof with a clatter. I saw him jump as clearly as if I had actually watched him.

Do I live in a different world from that occupied by those who can see with their physical eyes? Yes, in a way I do. But it is a beautiful, challenging world, filled with joy and tears, love and hate, triumph and failure. Though I cannot look at it in the same way others do, it is the same world that is occupied by the so-called sighted. My world, however, can be more rewarding in so many little ways.

"I'm looking for a Braille pattern for socks," I told the book adviser at the Virginia State Library for the Blind several years ago. "Don't ask me why I want to learn how to knit socks, but I do."

"Oh, that's easy, knowing you," she said. "It's just one more mountain to climb."

And what a rewarding climb it was as I sat with my dog at my feet and felt the good, honest Virginia wool turning into a thing of warmth and beauty under my fingers.

This is the story of my world, its mountains of triumph, its valleys of failure, its streams of love. As worlds go, it is a simple one. My mountains bear simple names, known only to those who love me, yet I have climbed them with pride.

It is the story of all those who have walked with me—my family, my friends, my teachers—but mostly it is about my animals, especially Lear, that gallant dog who devoted his life to serving me. They will live always in the depths of my memory, animals and people, giving me the blue of peace, the red of joy, and a rainbow of love.

1

"God Always Hears. . . "

Faith is to believe what we do not see; and the reward of this faith is to see what we believe.

SAINT AUGUSTINE

It was 1943. All over the world, people lived with fear, with death, with sorrow. Civilization was engulfed in the horror of the war, which, please God, would end all wars.

But for me, a five-year-old in rural Virginia, the war was only something I heard about as I sat on Mama's lap, smelling the pulp and ink of the newspaper as she read aloud.

It was something called rationing, which meant that Mama and my sister Fay couldn't get the sugar to make as much preserves as usual from the wild strawberries that grew free for the picking in almost all of the fields. It was the absence of cousins and neighbor boys, friends of my brother, all gone to that strange thing I couldn't quite understand, that mysterious thing called the war.

Always, too, there in the warm safety of the farmhouse was the unspoken knowledge, understood even by me, that soon, before the year was over, my brother, Lively, would have to go along with the others. I knew that sometimes people went to the war and never came back. And every night in my own way, I asked God to bring Lively back, "if he has to go at all." It was probably not much of a prayer, although it expressed my fear and hope. My secret hope was that surely something would keep him from having to go away. He had always been there, fifteen years older than I, pulling my pigtails, carrying me when I got tired, or bringing me little surprises from town. My big brother!

I am the youngest of four, the child of my parents' winter years. Inez is seven years older than I; Fay, seven years older than Inez; Lively one year older than Fay. It was almost as though I were an only child, except it was a lot more fun.

Fay was always there, another mother, to read to me, to teach my little hands how to do things that a sighted child can learn by imitation, but which must be painstakingly shown to a child who is blind.

Then, there was Inez, one of the most precious gifts that a little blind girl ever had. Fay and Lively were so much older than I that they were like bonus parents, there to love or to scold me, just always there. But Inez—or Nez, as she is still called—was different. She understood so much that the others couldn't, because Nez and I shared a special, rare bond:

Both of us were born blind, and although seven years separate us, we are almost like twins.

It isn't easy to explain, but Nez meant the difference between a world that could have seemed desolate and one that was filled with companionship and understanding.

Even today, society finds it hard to understand and accept the blind as equals. It isn't that people want to be unkind. On the contrary, they are often afraid of doing or saying the wrong thing. But fifty years ago, the blind were frequently objects of pity, shunned by society, or put on an isolated pedestal as someone special. No matter which group they fell into, life could be lonely, especially in rural areas.

I remember a day when I must have been about four. I was sitting under a tree out of the sight of my mother and a neighbor, but within earshot.

"Mrs. Staton," the neighbor said, "have you ever wondered why God gave you the burden of two blind children?"

"What in the world do you mean?" my mother asked, indignation in every carefully spaced syllable. "I love all four of my children, but my blind girls are a special gift. God gave them to me and Oscar to raise and educate. They're no burden."

I'm sure that that kind, caring neighbor sincerely meant to be sympathetic. I am equally sure that she told people "how well those girls get along." Yet, she felt that we were beings very different from the other children in the community.

Of course, I didn't understand the conversation. Not really. I didn't even know what a burden was, although I thought it wasn't something nice. Certainly I didn't fully understand the beautiful answer my mother had given. I felt a good, warm, tingly feeling in my stomach, though, the kind of sensation you have when you touch a baby or hear a Brahms symphony. Something rare and precious had touched my world.

Today, of course, Nez would be called a role model, but I just knew that I loved her. She read to me from Braille books. *The Little Colonel, Giant Scissors*, so many beloved titles, the very sound of which bring to mind long summer days with the breeze blowing through the trees and the trilling call of a cardinal. Her hands guided my tiny ones over the Braille alphabet, so that when I went to school I was way ahead of the other children of my age.

It was that magical thing called school that caused my great unhappiness.

We lived some seventy miles away from the residential school for the blind, a great distance in those days. Nez would leave for school in September and not return home until Christmas vacation. When she went back after Christmas, she wouldn't come home again until summer vacation. The happiest day of my life would be when she came home, and it seemed that the world must surely end the day she went back. I wanted to go, too, and no amount of explaining that I couldn't go until I was six would console me. Nez was there, and I wanted to go with her.

I had one consolation, and that was the animals. Everybody else in the house was so much older than I, so self-sufficient, but they, the animals, looked to me for love. I could pet them, and I could feed them. In short, although of course I didn't understand it then, they needed me.

Mama always said that I was talking before I could walk, my first words being, "Sly Boy catch groundhog." And she had always ended the story with, "and you haven't stopped talking since."

Sly, or Sly Boy as I called him, is the first animal I can remember. Dr. Sandridge, who had brought all of us into the world, had given him and his littermate Dallas to Lively when he was just a little boy. Lively remembered that he carried the puppies home in a bushel basket.

Dallas had been killed long before I was born, and although Sly was old enough to draw Social Security, he was there in all the slow independence that is the heritage of the hound. He was far too busy to take much time with a little girl, but he was my dog and I loved him.

I know now that we were really quite poor in the things the world considers riches, but I truly didn't know it then. I had Mama and Daddy, Nez, Fay, and Lively. I had Sly and all my cats. There were the baby chickens, hatched in the incubator warmed by a kerosene burner, and—joy of joys!—

sometimes delivered directly to us from a mail-order house.

It was my job to listen for the "ooga-ooga" of the little horn on the postman's mail truck. It signaled the exciting news that he had a package. Off one of the grownups would go to collect the long-awaited chicks while I jumped up and down in excitement.

Everybody held his breath as Mama determined if any had failed to make the trip alive. If I was especially good, I was allowed to hold one of the unbelievably small soft balls, which cheeped and squirmed in my hands. There was something about those helpless puffs that made me want to cry. They were so dear, so little, and even though it was just for a minute, one of them had been entrusted to me, a responsibility too wonderful for words.

It wasn't long after Nez had gone back to school after Christmas that year of 1943 that our neighbor Mrs. Franklin gave me the kitten. As I've said, there was Sly, and all the others, but until then I had never had anything alive that belonged to me and me alone. She was yellow, and if I'm honest, she was a scrawny little thing, but I didn't care—she was *mine.*

"What will you name her?" Mama asked.

Now, here is where I'm a bit vague. I have no idea where the name came from. It could have been from a book, or maybe from some program I'd heard on the big battery-operated radio in our living room, but wherever it came from, I promptly replied, "Mouser."

So Mouser became a part of the family. She slept with the barn cats, but every morning she presented herself at the back door to be fed, and she was the first thing I heard when I came into the warm kitchen.

"She's speaking to you," Mama would say as Mouser's squeaky little meow greeted me.

It is a learned response, of course, that "*meow*" or "*woof*" to get the attention of the blind mistress or master, but for me it was the most wonderful sound I'd ever heard. Mouser knew I couldn't see, and I thought she was the smartest cat on earth.

"I want to take her for a ride," I told Mama one day. "I'm going to put her in my doll carriage."

"Why don't I fix her a nice box so you can pull her behind you?" Mama suggested. "You might bump the carriage into something."

So Mouser had her own private coach, which I pulled behind me all over the yard. Every now and then we'd hit an unexpected bump or rock, over would go the coach, and out would tumble Mouser.

Today I truly question not only her intelligence but also her sanity. Faced with such a situation, the average, reasonably intelligent cat would have taken the providence-given opportunity and run for safety, if not for her life. Not Mouser. She would sit there patiently waiting until I had righted her equipage, picked her up, settled her again, and off we'd go.

It was a cold morning in spring when I rushed to the warmth of the kitchen to find that Mouser wasn't waiting as usual.

"But I want her to come," I said in that obstinate way of a child. "I want her to come right now, Mama. I'm lonesome."

"I know," Mama said, "but come and eat your breakfast. There's oatmeal with raisins."

Although it was one of my very favorite breakfasts, the day held no joy. Down deep inside, I felt a sick worry that never quite left no matter what I did.

Late that afternoon I stood in the yard where we had played together so many mornings, warmed by the winter sun. Even though it was spring, the afternoon was as cold as I felt inside.

Every Sunday when we went to service at the little country church, the minister or one of the deacons would pray, "And, dear Heavenly Father, please bring our boys back safely."

Well, if it worked for our boys, why not for our cats? So, there in the cold and wind, surrounded by the evening sounds of the cows and the smell of the supper fire, I knelt on one of the very rocks that had wrecked Mouser's coach so many times, and prayed.

"Dear Heavenly Father, please bring our Mouser back safe, and please, too, dear Heavenly Father, don't let Brother have to go to the Army. Amen. I'll be good."

"I've already said my prayers," I told Mama that night as she slipped the soft flannel nightgown over my head.

"Now, Phyllis," she said. "When?"

"This evening. I asked God to bring Mouser home. Do you think He heard, Mama?"

"God always hears our prayers," she said, hugging me just a little tighter than usual.

"Where is Mouser?" I asked the next morning when I ran into the kitchen.

"Eat your breakfast, and then I have something to tell you," Mama said.

I hardly tasted the eggs with bread that had been thickly spread with Mama's own good butter and toasted in the oven. I had a sick, strange feeling that she was going to tell me something I didn't want to hear, some grown-up thing I didn't want to know. Still, God did hear prayers, I told myself.

"I'm sorry," Mama said when I had finished, "but Mouser's dead. She followed the big cats, and a car killed her. Brother found her late yesterday, and he buried her in the yard under the big tree where you like to play. But listen. God gave you the nicest present, because the barn cat, Patsy, had kittens, and Daddy says you can have whichever one you want for your very own. As soon as it's old enough to leave Patsy, we'll bring it to the house."

For one minute I was rocked by the worst feeling of sorrow I've ever experienced. Mouser was my first real loss, and somehow I knew the world would never be quite the same. I had lost my innocence, my childlike conviction that nothing could ever hurt me. Of course I didn't know that then. I only knew how I felt. But I never once blamed God. Mama had assured me that He heard, and there was no doubt in my mind that He had. The new kitten wouldn't be Mouser, but God had given it to me, and I would love it.

I have often thought about how hard it must have been for my mother to leave me to the wisdom and care of God, content in the certainty that somehow He would bring me through that first experience with death. What a temptation it must have been for her to tell me that sometimes God didn't answer prayers, or even to ignore what I had told her.

She knew, though, that soon I would be going to a school far away from her, where I would have to depend on my relationship with God. I have sometimes wondered, too, if some deeply buried instinct warned her that before I even finished high school she would be gone, and Daddy would be almost helpless as the result of a stroke. They wouldn't be there to protect me, and I would need the sustaining knowledge that God hears.

That day, of course, I knew nothing of such things. I only knew that my friend was gone, and that we would never play again, never snuggle together in the big rocker for a nap.

Tears ran down my cheeks, and then I remembered what Mama had said. No, the new kitten wouldn't be Mouser—nobody could ever be Mouser—but still I felt comforted in a sad sort of way. I would have a new friend, and we could find new things to do.

"Maybe I'll want a little boy cat this time," I said. "But first will you show me Mouser's grave?"

As she took my hand, I remembered the other part of my prayer.

"Mama"—I spoke softly, almost afraid to voice the thought—"will Brother have to go to the war?"

"I'm afraid so." I could hear the hoarse sound of tears in her words.

"But God will bring him back," I said, although, to tell the truth, I was still afraid. *But He always hears*, I silently reminded myself.

2

Christmas Magic

Unselfish and noble actions are the most radiant pages in the biography of souls.

DAVID THOMAS

If that year of 1943 was one of strife and despair for the world, it was one of change, of hope, indeed of magic for me.

The world of a child is often filled with a secret wonder or fear, which, like the sound of fairy voices in the still summer night, or the sense of something alien at midnight, may belong to her and her alone. It is made up of so many things that are known only to a child, or to one whose spirit can find its way back to that world.

There were the warm summer days filled with the scent of flowers and the sound of sheets blowing on the line. There were the smoky days of fall as the night drew in early and the fire crackled in the kitchen range. There was the first snow, covering the earth with soft, crunchy cold. All these memories, along with so many more, paint the portrait of my early childhood—a time of carefree love that was the prelude to that longed-for adventure called school.

I can't help smiling at the tears shed by a mother who deposits her child at his or her school for the first day. She is as close as her telephone, and that night she can tuck her darling safely into his or her own bed. Not so, for the blind or deaf children of fifty years ago.

Today, of course, the public schools must provide special classes for the handicapped and most handicapped children live at home. In those days, however, deaf and blind children were educated from kindergarten through high school in residential schools, often far away from the pupil's home.

In Virginia, the School for the Deaf and Blind is located in Staunton. Actually it is two schools, one for the blind and one for the deaf, sharing the same superintendent, maintenance staff, and health service. The enrollment for both schools has dwindled alarmingly since the children have been mainstreamed into the public schools, and today the schools are in imminent danger of being closed, which I think would be a tragedy.

These days, the pupils go home every weekend, but fifty years ago parents relinquished their children to the care of the houseparents and teachers for months, usually seeing them only at the Christmas vacation and during the summer. In many ways parents actually gave their children up, but it was worth it.

Education, of course, is essential for all children, but for blind children it is doubly important, for they must learn so many more skills than the average child is taught in school. Even now, at the end of the twentieth century with its computers and a so-called enlightened public, the blind often find it difficult to obtain meaningful employment and social acceptance. The residential school still helps to open the door to society through the give-and-take that can be achieved only through interaction with others who are blind. There is no pity or rejection from one's peers, because all share the same problem. The school for the blind also develops special skills, such as Braille music and sports, that are geared to the needs of the blind. Yet, it cannot be denied that it was hard for both parents and children to leave each other for such a long time.

It was toward this separation from my parents, home, and pets that I longed. How hard it must have been for my mother to give up two of her children, especially her "baby." Still, that is what she did—first Nez, and then me. She knew that it was our only chance to get the education that was essential if we were to live normal lives.

"Little girls who go away to school have to learn to dress themselves," she told me just before my sixth birthday, in what was probably a last-ditch effort to keep me from wanting to go to school in January, following my birthday on the first of December.

"Okay," I said as I snuggled down under the quilts to think about it.

It had been harder than cracking walnuts to persuade Mama and Daddy to get permission from Mr. Healy, the superintendent of the school, to enroll me after the Christmas vacation, and I wasn't about to let a few buttons spoil things.

"Look, Mama," I said bursting into the warmth of the kitchen the next morning. "I did it all except my sash. That doesn't count."

And with that, I turned around with all the assurance of the chairman of the board who secretly fears the stockholders will vote against him.

"That doesn't count," she agreed, with what I now know was resignation in her voice, as she started to tie the bow.

"I'm going to school," I told Sly. "You know this is my birthday, and I'm six years old, and I'm going to school."

I had wanted to tell Gray Boy, the gray tomcat I had chosen after Mouser died, but like most toms, he was nowhere to be found when you wanted him.

The December sun felt warm against my face, and I wondered if I'd get by with it if I took my scarf off. I hated scarves. They weren't quite so bad since Mama had cut my hair, another concession to school. Short hair is so much easier for a little girl to manage, and Mama and Fay were determined that I was going to manage as much as I could by myself. But short hair or not, I hated that scarf that covered up my ears, hated it almost as much as I hated the angora mittens that kept me from seeing with my fingers.

"I'm going to school," I repeated, just to be sure Sly had heard. "I'm not going to miss anybody, not even you, old dog." And I gave him a hug, which he grudgingly accepted.

There in the warm December sun, with my arms around his neck, smelling the clean doggie smell and feeling his collar against my cheek, I meant it. It was only in the night, when I awoke to hear the wind speaking of the cold, lonely dark, that I felt a frozen little lump deep inside me. Soon I would be in a strange bed, surrounded by strange sounds and strange smells and strange people.

Of course, I had been there when we had gone to bring Nez home or to take her back, but that wasn't the same. I had been to the dormitory room with a row of beds along each side and a row of metal lockers at each end, but that had been in the daytime, when people were everywhere, talking and laughing and playing. What would it be like at night? Would the same wind speak of the same cold, dark things? And what if I had to get up? I knew that the bathroom was across the wide hall that ran from the front of the building to the back. And lying safe at home, I wondered if strange, quiet things would lurk there in that hall just waiting for a little girl to leave her warm bed and dare to come out.

But now, in the sunlit day, I was sure of myself, standing there hugging Sly with the cool winter breeze blowing the hated scarf.

"I'm going to learn Braille, and I'm going to play the piano, and I'll come back and play at the church, but you can't come, because dogs can't go to church."

Today, they sound like such small ambitions, yet they were the first steps toward what I have become. The first steps toward the woman. Ambitions that were achieved with more effort than the child could have imagined.

But as I gave Sly one final pat and skipped toward the house where I knew Fay was baking my birthday cake—chocolate, with chocolate icing trimmed with black walnuts—the day, the world was mine. After all, it was a long time until January.

I had already opened my presents—three new dresses with panties to match, and four long flannel nightgowns, all made by Mama and Fay at the old Singer sewing machine.

"When we go to town before Christmas, we'll get you some new shoes," Mama said as she adjusted the little panties, which were made to just peep from beneath my dress. I was going to school in style!

"Santa Claus is coming early this year," I told Nez as we snuggled together in bed. We had gone that day all the way to Staunton, a whole seventy miles, an incredibly long way to me, to bring her home for the Christmas vacation.

"Why is Santa coming early?" she asked, cuddling me close. "Have you been that good?"

"I don't think I have," I said honestly, "but Daddy says Santa will bring my presents early so I'll have longer to play with them before I go to school. Do you think he will come early?"

"If Daddy says so," she said. "I'll be glad to see Lively, won't you?"

"Well, I've missed him since he went to the Army," I confessed. "But I don't think I'll tell him. Brothers are nice, but don't you think they can be a lot of trouble sometimes?"

"Maybe," she half agreed. "But we're glad he's coming for Christmas, anyhow, aren't we?"

Then, suddenly, I heard it—a thud and thump coming from the living room. Like most farm families, we went to bed early, all of us, and I knew it must be, had to be, only one person down there.

"It's him! It's him! Nez, it's Santa—it really is!"

"Shh!" she whispered. "You don't want him to know you're awake."

And there in the cold December night, the world was suddenly touched with magic. Santa Claus, that strange old man who surely must exist, but who just might not, was there, right under the same roof. I could hear him. I could almost smell the strange place he had come from. He was there, making a special trip just because I was going to school!

There was one last especially loud thud, followed by a silence during which I didn't dare breathe. Suppose he had heard me? I had been read a story about Santa taking back presents from a little girl who had peeped through the door. Then, from the yard came the faint sound of a bell moving along the lane. It grew fainter and fainter until the night was still again. . . .

It was Daddy, of course, although to this day I don't know where he got that little bell, which to my mind sounded just the way a sleigh bell must surely sound.

It is still one of my most cherished memories, the very embodiment of the spirit of that magical love that is the true essence of Christmas. I can't remember what he brought, but I will always remember the thrill of that night when, unmarred by unbelief, which would come with association with older children, I knew beyond a doubt that Santa existed.

I cherish the memory today, because of the love and imagination of my family who understood the importance of giving a blind child a realistic "picture" of Santa Claus, one last little special gift before she entered the world of reality.

For those children who are blind, the department-store Santas are only voices in the babble and confusion around them, totally lacking realism. And I'd bet my Bing Crosby Christmas album that there has never been a church Santa who has been able to fool a blind child. There aren't, after all, whiskers to disguise his voice.

This, though, was different. I had heard him, right there in my own house, had listened as his sleigh disappeared to who knew where. And so each year I remember, and feel again, the love of those dear ones who will be with me always, even though miles or death separate us.

3

World of Wonders

I will instruct thee and teach thee in the way which thou shalt go; I will counsel thee with my eye upon thee.

PSALMS 32:8

The next few days passed with the speed of a rabbit running from Sly, or that of the sorghum molasses as it poured from the pitcher on cold mornings. One minute it would seem that the time was going so fast I couldn't breathe, and the next I thought that the second of January, a Sunday that year, would never come.

Lively had come home on furlough, full of stories, just a couple of days after Nez had come home from school, and the house was filled with talk and laughter. He picked me up, hugged me, asked what had happened to my hair, put me down, only to pick me up again for another hug.

He brought presents for everybody, but the only thing I can remember was a cloth drawstring bag filled with pecans still in the shell. I was delighted at how easy it was to shell them using the nutcracker that he brought with them. I didn't find it quite so easy to pick them out, although I didn't tell anybody that.

I just about knocked Nez unconscious with a toy gun while we were acting out a story inspired by one of our Nancy Drew books. I truly don't remember whether I was the good girl or the bad one, but Mama warned that the game would promptly be brought to a halt if any more violence occurred.

And so the days moved on, one by one, until that longed-for, and feared, day arrived.

It was a bright day of cold wind and warm sun, without a cloud in the sky, according to my second cousin Ronnie, who had come with his parents, Evelyn and Julian, to take us to Staunton, since we didn't have a car.

"I'm glad I don't have to go away to school," Ronnie said as Julian helped Daddy carry my suitcases to the car.

"You're just jealous," I said, although, to tell the truth, I was beginning to regret it myself. It was rather like the way you feel on a cold morning, snuggled under the covers, even though you know the day has something exciting just waiting for you to get up for.

"I am not," he said. And then, to my delight and amazement, he added, "Well, not much, anyhow. Come on, they're ready."

And he reached to take my hand.

"I'll be there in a minute," I said, pulling my hand away.

I had already told them good-bye, the cows, the two farm horses, Prince and Sam, my fur friends, and there was only Gray Boy, curled on a chair next to the stove in the kitchen. I had put it off until the last minute, because deep inside it seemed that as long as I didn't tell him good-bye, I might not be going.

"Come on, Phyllie," Daddy said, using his pet name for me, a name used most often by his sister, my Aunt Laura.

"I love you, Gray Boy," I whispered, giving him one last hug, only to run back and plant a kiss between his ears. "You be a good cat, and remember to keep the mice out of the pantry."

The car was crowded as we all squeezed ourselves in. There were Mama and Daddy, Evelyn and Julian, and Ronnie, Nez, and, to my joy, Fay.

Until now Fay had taken neighborhood jobs, such as sitting with Mrs. Smith who lived up the road, and who, to my mind, was about a hundred years old. Now, though, Fay was leaving home to take a job at the School for the Blind, operating the switchboard, something too complicated for me to even think about. She was going with me. Fay would be there, Nez would be there, and I wouldn't be alone.

I didn't think about it then, of course, but although I wouldn't be alone, my parents would. Lively had gone back a week earlier, so that in the space of a week, all their children were gone. Today I think about how lonely that house must have seemed when they came home that night. I can imagine them lighting the lamps and building up the fires, there alone for the first time since Lively's birth, and I marvel again at the courage they showed in allowing all three of us girls to find our own lives.

But I knew nothing of such grown-up things as I put on my new nightgown that night and climbed into my bed.

There were sixteen of us—the little girls, we were called. We all slept in a long room that ran almost the whole length of the right side of the building on the ground floor. Across the wide hall was a practice room with a little sewing room behind it; the lavatory with a utility sink and four commodes; the shower room with basins, a tub, and a shower; the playroom; and Mrs. Keister's room. Across from her room, and next door to the dormitory, was the room where Mrs. Keister's student helpers slept.

Mrs. Keister was my housemother. In those days the housemothers—one for the little girls and one for the big girls—lived at the school and were on duty twenty-four hours a day. They had one half-day a week, and one Sunday every two weeks, off duty. Although I don't know for sure, I have the feeling they were paid about one hundred dollars a month. Generally they were widows or unmarried ladies, the latter often unkindly called old maids. I expect that a woman—or a man for that matter—who was divorced wouldn't have been considered for the job, though it seems strange today.

From time to time, I heard hair-raising stories of cruelty, especially from the boys, and no doubt some of them were true. It would stand to reason that people took such a job either because they had a genuine concern for children or because they couldn't find a job anywhere else. Also, such responsibility and confinement would surely bring out the worst of personality flaws.

Nez and I were fortunate. I had Mrs. Keister, and she had Mrs. French, both widows who genuinely loved children and who brought the love of God to their charges both by word and example.

Mrs. Keister was Nez's first housemother, too, and she and my mother developed a friendship that was to continue between our families until her death. Her husband had died when her only daughter, Edith, was just a baby. Jobs for women, especially a woman with a child to raise, were scarce in those days, but Mrs. Keister worked as a private-duty nurse in order to support herself and Edith.

It would have seemed that things were finally working out well for them. Edith was working as a secretary and Mrs. Keister was keeping house for her when, suddenly, Edith died of

an unsuspected heart condition. Mrs. Keister went to work at
the Ohio School for the Blind, and then the Virginia school,
where she had been working for probably about twenty years
when I became a pupil.

So, the mother deprived of her only child became the
mother to countless children who, in a special way, belonged
to her more than to their own mothers. I know that in many
ways she shaped my character more than my own mother,
simply because I spent more time with her. Often, even now,
I say a prayer of thanks for that life given with so much love
to the rearing of other women's children.

"Good night, little girls," she said on that first night, and I
heard the click of the light switch located high on the wall
outside the dormitory door.

It was still early, and I could hear the big girls in their dormitory upstairs, talking and laughing. I knew that Nez was
somewhere up there, and I wished that I could have slept
near her. I had stayed with her until suppertime when I'd
been introduced to my partner, another of Mrs. Keister's girls,
whose name was Ellen Shiflet. We all had partners, usually a
slightly older girl with a little girl, as we lined up to go to the
dining room.

To get to the dining room, which we shared with the children from the Department for the Deaf, we had to go upstairs
in our building, Montague Hall, and across a connection
porch. It was cold that night, and as we went across the
porch, I could smell coal smoke from the furnaces along Beverley Street and from the nearby railroad. From the dining
room came the smell of cabbage, and I felt my first pang of
homesickness. Mama would just be taking the corn bread out
of the oven, or maybe even a blackberry roll made with the
berries she had canned the summer before. The house would
be warm, and Gray Boy would be rubbing around her ankles,
hoping for something to eat.

The dining room was noisy, and everything tasted so different. We stood behind our chairs until a bell rang, signaling the blessing. We all sang it together, with the deaf students signing the words.

Now I lay in my little bed with the covers tucked in so tight that I could hardly move. I listened to the sounds from upstairs growing softer and softer, until Montague Hall was quiet except for the hiss of the radiators and an occasional rush of water as somebody flushed somewhere in the building, which suddenly seemed as big as the whole world.

From somewhere outside a clock struck, and I counted ten. I had learned to count, listening to the clock on a shelf in the kitchen at home, and I knew that meant it was ten o'clock. Nez had told me that at ten o'clock, Mr. Ham, the night watchman, would go to the basement and turn the heat off until five-thirty the next morning. As I listened, sure enough, I heard the outside door to the basement open, and a squeaking sound. Then the door closed, and I heard his steps disappear along the walk.

A spatter of sleet tapped at the windows, and I found myself wondering if it was sleet—or some strange creature of the night trying to find its way in. Overhead, between the ceiling and the next floor, I heard the stealthy movement of claws. I knew what that was. I was from the country, after all, and I wasn't afraid of a mouse—well, not much anyhow. Still, I was glad he was up there.

I burrowed deeper under the covers, and almost held my breath as something moved stealthily along the hall. Then I breathed again as I heard the jingle of keys, which had already become familiar. It was Mrs. Keister, going to lock the door that led to the lower porch. No doubt I had been exposed to too much Nancy Drew!

I touched the barrette that still held my hair back from my face. Mama had put it there that morning, and I let my fingers linger where hers had rested. Tomorrow, of course, Lois, one of the student helpers, would take it out and rearrange my hair.

One big tear, then another, made its way along my nose and onto the pillow. I knew how lucky I was to have Nez and Fay close. When Nez had started school, she had been all by herself. Another fat tear found its way to the collar of my nightgown, this one for her. That was probably the first time in my life I had felt the pain and sorrow of somebody else. Mostly, though, I felt sad for myself there in that strange bed whose sheets smelled so different from those at home, dried in the sun and the wind. I wanted to go home, and I felt like howling.

From the railroad came the puff-puff of a steam engine, its whistle seeming to echo my loneliness. Surely the whole world must be lonely on this cold, dreary night.

Then, I heard it. At first I thought I must be imagining it, that sound, so familiar, so dear. But as I listened, I knew it was real. Somewhere outside, a dog was barking.

It wasn't Sly—I knew that. Sly was far away, sleeping in the hay, or maybe sniffing out the winter lair of a fox. No, it wasn't him. But as I listened to the familiar *yo-yo-yo yo-yo-yo,* it seemed that in some strange way he was sending me a message. It was as though, in some way known only to his kind, he had communicated with his brother or sister there where I was, sending me a message of hope and love.

I love you, old dog, I said in my head. *I love you.*

The building had grown cold, and the tears had dried on my cheeks. Tomorrow I would start school, would meet my teacher, would get a chance to play with the other little girls.

Tomorrow, I told the dog, just before I fell asleep.

4

A Friend in the Night

*The guardian angels of life sometimes fly so high as
to be beyond our sight, but they are always looking
down upon us.*

JOHN PAUL RICHTER

As I opened my eyes on that Friday, January seventh, it was
with a mixture of anticipation and a dull feeling of loneliness.

It was the last day of my first week in school, and although
it still held that bright promise of something new and exciting, I was a little disappointed. Nez had worked hard through
the summer, holding daily "school" in the upstairs hall with
the warm breeze blowing through the door to the upper
porch. I could read and write the Braille alphabet, something
I considered a wonderful accomplishment, although it would
be several years, Nez had explained, before I learned all the
contractions.

The Braille "cell" is made up of six dots, three down and two across. All the letters and contractions are formed from these six dots. Braille can be written using a slate and stylus, simply a guide made up of lines of cells. The paper is placed in this frame or guide so that the dots can be punched with the stylus. There is one little snag. In order to turn the paper over to feel the dots reading from left to right, the dots must be punched in reverse, from right to left.

To a small child, of course, this presents no serious problem, since the whole thing is new. For the older child or adult who has just lost her sight, however, it must seem the height of confusion.

Even then, of course, we had Braille writers, machines with six keys representing the six dots, which mercifully wrote the right way up. But to this day, the slate and stylus provide the cheapest and simplest way to write Braille, since they go anywhere in a small amount of space. I have what sometimes seems like a house full of technical equipment, including a minicomputer with the six Braille keys, but if I mislay my little slate and favorite stylus, I turn everything upside down until they are found.

I am often amused when people say, "But how on earth can a child learn such a complicated thing?" The blind child learns Braille just as other children learn to read and write. Braille seems no harder to her than reading and writing seems to any other child who has never learned those skills. First the child learns the alphabet, and next the various contractions that make up the Braille code. If it wasn't contracted, Braille would be so cumbersome that it wouldn't be practical. As it is, Braille books take up an enormous amount of room. The King James version of the Bible, for instance, is made up of eighteen enormous volumes.

"But why don't you use those wonderful recordings?" people often ask today. Why indeed? I'm not sure I can say. Of course I use recorded material; I use computer electronic books too. Still, there is something about feeling the words under my fingers that is almost mystical. It is the feel, the smell, the very texture of the paper, something personal and special, that has always touched a chord of harmony somewhere deep inside me. And that magical world was within my tiny hands.

"I know your sister is teaching you to read," Miss Eisenburg, my kindergarten teacher, said, "but I have a lot of other things to teach you too."

For me, though, nothing, not even the singing games, would ever be as wonderful as those tiny rough dots, which said things, sometimes even things like Bible verses, that somebody had said years and years ago. Truly, I was disappointed not to be spending all my time reading, but Miss Eisenburg was right—there were plenty of other things to learn.

There were the pegboards with their round and square holes. There were walks in the cold winter air listening to the birdsongs that reminded me of home and Gray Boy, who was always stalking some poor bird no matter how well we fed him. And there were the games—"The Farmer in the Dell," "London Bridge," "Here We Go Round the Mulberry Bush"— and not a single soul to tell me I couldn't play because I was blind.

I did love school even though it wasn't all reading and writing.

But then there were the nights. Cold, quiet hours with the old building groaning in the wind, and mice—or maybe even rats—scurrying around in the ceiling. Around me I could hear the others sometimes moving, sometimes whimpering in their sleep, reminding me of Sly as he chased a rabbit or a fox through the fields of his dreams.

Occasionally somebody would turn over and knock her

doll out of bed with a loud crash that would silence the scurrying overhead, at least for a little while. I had left my dolls at
home to "keep Mama company," but in the cold quiet of the
night, I wished for Jane, my doll that was as big as a baby and
emitted a sound that passed for a cry when you tipped her
back and forth. If I just had Jane!

Still, I told myself yet again on that early Friday morning, I
was at school and I was learning. I was learning so I would be
just like Nez.

I heard the familiar squeak as Mr. Ham turned on the heat,
and I snuggled deeper under the covers. It would be a while
yet before I heard Mrs. Keister's alarm clock, and still longer
before she and her helpers, Lois and Lucille, came to get us
up. All three of them had been enormously proud to find my
bed dry on my first morning, and I had been enormously
indignant to think that they would think it wouldn't be.

"I didn't think you'd be wet," Mrs. Keister said, giving my
cheek a pat, "but sometimes little girls have an accident in a
strange place."

And they hadn't checked again.

I lay listening to the radiators, a tapping, gurgling sound
that made me think of the coffeepot at home.

Today I would finish my first school week, and just as I
turned that thought around like a tasty peppermint, I gave an
enormous sneeze. It probably woke everybody up, which
didn't really matter, because just as I gave the second sneeze,
I heard the click of the dormitory light, accompanied by Mrs.
Keister's brisk voice.

"Here, here, child. Are you catching cold?"

And she laid the back of her hand on my forehead.

"Oh, no, ma'am," I said in a voice that even to me sounded
a little like one of the crows that picked for corn in the barn-
yard.

"Do you feel all right?" she asked, handing me my socks,

which matched my dress. That was something I had to take on faith, because although all my dresses felt different, all those little socks were the same color so far as I was concerned.

"Oh, I feel fine," I said.

I knew that little girls who were sick had to go to the infirmary, and I knew all about the infirmary. Or at least I thought I did. The day before, right in the middle of dropping "London Bridge," I had been interrupted by Mrs. Covile, the principal, who said the nurse wanted me in the infirmary.

"But I'm not sick," I had protested.

"Of course you aren't," she had agreed, taking my hand, which had suddenly grown quite cold. "That's why she wants you. She's going to give you something called a vaccination to keep you from getting sick."

And off we had gone, her heels clicking and my shoes squeaking over the concrete.

It had started to rain as we went along the bridge, which was actually a system of connection porches, on our way to the infirmary. It was on the top floor of an old brick building that housed the kitchen on the ground floor and the dining room on the second.

They couldn't fool me. I knew what a vaccination was. I'd had one in Lynchburg back in the fall, and it had hurt.

"I don't think I want to go," I repeated as we started up the steep flight of steps that led to the infirmary.

"I know," Mrs. Covile said, "but you're in school now, and so you're a big girl. Your sister had to be vaccinated when she first came to school."

That did it. If Nez had done it, I'd do it, too, if it killed me. And they had said it would keep me from getting sick, hadn't they?

Well, it hadn't worked so well, I thought the next morning as I turned for Mrs. Keister to tie the big bow at the back of my dress. Because, although I wouldn't admit it to a soul, I thought I just might be getting sick. As I sneezed again, I would have given anything to climb back under the covers and go back to sleep, but Mrs. Keister had mentioned the infirmary, and I might get stuck again if I went up there.

So I gave what I hoped was a quiet sniffle and made my somewhat staggering way down the hall to the bathroom.

"Phyllis is sick," Fay Wine, the student who waited on the little girls' table in the dining room, said as she touched my forehead and felt my pulse. Fay was one of the students who, although they were legally blind, had a lot of sight. She had taken me to Mrs. Keister as soon as the bell had rung to signal that supper was over.

"Come here," Mrs. Keister said, taking me on her lap and popping a thermometer into my mouth.

"She didn't eat anything," Fay continued, "and I noticed how flushed she was. She never eats much, but tonight she didn't even drink her milk." And she reached to give my hand a pat. One of the wonderful things about the residential school for the blind was all that love and help the students gave one another. When a new pupil came, the others usually helped in any way they could. After all, they knew what it was like to leave a warm, loving family and find yourself in a strange place, surrounded by strange people and even strange food.

"Her temperature is one hundred and three," Mrs. Keister said as she read the thermometer. "I'll have to send you to the infirmary, child." She put me on Fay's lap and went to her desk to write the nurse's "ticket" with my name, the date, and complaint.

"But I don't want to go." I buried my head in Fay's lap. "I'm not very sick, honest."

"Go upstairs and tell her sister Inez that Phyllis has to go to the infirmary, and they'll have to keep her," Mrs. Keister told one of the other girls.

Then I really did put up a howl. It had been bad enough to have to go up there to get my vaccination, but I'd been able to leave when the nurse had finished. Now Mrs. Keister was saying I'd have to stay.

"It won't be long," Nez promised when she got there. But I could hear something that sounded suspiciously like tears in her voice. She hugged me. "I'll come to see you, and we'll tell Sister Fay, and she'll come to see you too."

"Maybe they won't keep me," I said, blowing my nose.

After all, I didn't know what it meant to have a temperature of one hundred and three.

"Don't count on that," Nez said, "but it probably won't be for long."

"This is Miss Carson," Nez said a few minutes later as we stood in the little dispensary at the front of the infirmary.

"Where do you feel sick?" Miss Carson asked, lifting me onto a stool that seemed about a mile tall.

"I'm not sick," I protested. Maybe there was still a chance she would let me go back with the others.

"The thermometer says you are." She looked in my left ear and then the right. "Let's look at your throat." She held my tongue down. "There's the trouble." She dropped the tongue depressor into the trash can with a little bang. "Your tonsils are as red as fire. You come and stay with us tonight. Your sister can tuck you in," she added as I clung to Nez's hand.

The bed was big, and high, and felt cold. Later, I was to learn that I was in a room with six beds in it, although just then I was the only one there. I didn't want to be left in that big room that smelled like the disinfectant Mama used in the brooder house. I wondered if there would be little creatures running around in the ceiling here.

"Kiss your sister good night, and take this little pill for me," Miss Carson said, and I heard her set a glass on the table that fitted over the bed. "Do you have to go to the bathroom?"

"No, ma'am," I said, although I sort of thought I did.

"If you do, there's a little pot right at the foot of your bed." She handed me a pill that didn't feel very little to me.

Well, that was a relief, because I'd been wondering just what I'd do about the bathroom, but somehow I hadn't wanted to ask.

The pill went down with a gulp, and before I knew just what was happening I was left alone.

I finally managed to make a little nest of warmth for myself, but no matter how hard I tried, a tear kept sliding down my nose every few minutes. Miss Carson had given me a glass of grapefruit juice with the pill, and it had left a bitter, puckery feeling in my mouth. And I thought of home and a glass of buttermilk, cool and somehow sweet and tart all at the same time.

From the dispensary came the squeak of the desk chair and the slow click-click of the typewriter. Rain tapped at the window, and an airplane buzzed through the night sky. I wondered if that same plane would make its way over our house at home, so that Mama and Daddy and Gray Boy would hear it too. Maybe the world wasn't so big after all.

And from far off came the bark of the dog who sounded like Sly, offering his usual good night.

"Good night, old dog," I said aloud, because, after all, there wasn't anybody else in the room to hear.

5

Ghosts of the Past

The true past departs not; no truth or goodness realized by man ever died, or can die...

THOMAS CARLYLE

The next days and nights seemed unreal, filled with strange sounds and smells and hands. Even today I'm not sure what was reality and what the stuff of fever-induced dreams. It must have been around the fifth day, Wednesday, that things became less confused, and I realized that although I had thought I knew all about the infirmary before I had been admitted Friday night, I'd been wrong.

It was one of the original school buildings. It had been built just after the Civil War, when the state had had hardly enough money to feed the pupils. The building was solid enough, I suppose, but it totally lacked the architectural charm of Main Hall, with its broad front steps and columns.

But there was more than a lack of physical beauty, which, after all, meant nothing to a six-year-old who was totally blind. Looking back now, years later, I still find it difficult to describe.

There was a feeling, a sense of despair almost, that seemed to pervade the whole building. Of course, it could have been a reflection of my own frustration at being kept in what almost amounted to isolation, except for the visits of my sisters. Over the years, though, others have mentioned the same feeling in varying degrees of intensity.

I believe that events and emotions leave something akin to an echo reverberating in a place. Contrary to popular belief, this can leave joy as well as sadness or violence stamped on a site, and many realtors would agree with me. Whatever the cause, it is an established fact that some houses or buildings are "happy" while others aren't. That grim old building was definitely not happy. I am convinced that it echoed the sorrow of my sisters in spirit who had lain there over the years.

Much has been said about the lot of women in the last century, but if the lot of women in general was a sad one, it was all too often one of unbelievable despair for women who were blind. How many girls lay in that very room, thinking about the future, knowing it would be spent in the home of some grudging relative or in an institution where they would spend their days in a void?

Of course, some of them found jobs of a sort, and some may have found a loving husband, but they were the exceptions. Most had left home and family hoping for the fulfillment of the promise of a useful life, but I imagine it didn't take many years for them to realize that that hope was empty.

As I lay in that infirmary, my young self knew nothing of such things, but the woman is convinced that they—those lonely, often disillusioned girls—left something of themselves behind. And often, when I experience a little triumph, I think of them, those who succeeded, and those who, through no fault of their own, failed. And my triumph is theirs, because in a way they paved the way for me. Usually I regret the passing of something old, but I felt little sorrow when in the late 1960s that building fell to the wrecking ball.

Of all the infirmary routines, I hated naptime the most. I had never been into naps. Curious little creature that I was, I suppose I was afraid I might miss something. The idea of the nurse pulling the shades and leaving me shut in by myself for two hours, from two to four, was almost unbearable. The nights were bad enough.

I say "by myself," but that isn't quite accurate. Sometime during those confused days, I had acquired two roommates. They were scant comfort, though, because they were both totally deaf and unable to speak. I could hear the rustle of the sheets as they signed away, talking to each other, and it made me even more lonely.

I wanted to "go downstairs," the accepted expression for being allowed to go back to the dormitory, but it wasn't to be.

"Dr. Bradford is here to see you," Mrs. Lotts, the head nurse, said on Friday.

I think he must have been there during that period of confusion, but I don't remember it.

"How are you, Mary Jane?" he asked as Mrs. Lotts undid the top buttons on my nightgown so he could listen to my heart.

Nez had told me all about Dr. Bradford, so I knew he called all the little girls Mary Jane. This didn't mean that we weren't individuals to him. On the contrary, he could remember years later just what had been wrong with "Mary Jane," and what bearing it might have on her current complaint.

At that time, of course, I was what might be called a blank sheet of paper, since he had no past history to guide him, and he seemed puzzled, even to me.

"You say her temperature goes up every afternoon?" he asked.

"That's right, Doctor," Mrs. Lotts said.

"How's your appetite, Mary Jane?" he asked me as he did up the buttons of my gown.

"I'm hungry," I said honestly.

"She's been on liquids for several days, Doctor," Mrs. Lotts told him.

"Well, let's give her something light. How does that sound?"

It sounded good. At least, I thought it did. But I found myself wondering what something light meant.

"Maybe cream of wheat," he added, and my spirits fell. I disliked cream of wheat almost as much as I disliked grapefruit juice, but I didn't say so.

"When can I go downstairs?" I asked as I heard them starting toward the door.

"Not until your temperature goes down and stays down for a day or two," he said, coming back to lay a hand on my cheek.

And so the days passed, one so like the other that sometimes I couldn't count them. Then what I considered a happening almost too wonderful to describe occurred. Another little blind girl got sick. It must have been about the third week I was in the infirmary that I heard Miss Carson coming along the hall, and she was talking to somebody.

"I'm going to put you in the room with Phyllis Staton," she was saying. "You know her, don't you?"

"No, ma'am. She just came after Christmas, and I was late getting back from home. She'd already gone to the infirmary when I got back."

"Well, you're just about the same age," Miss Carson said, opening the door. "Phyllis, I've brought you some company. This is Shirley Lyons. She's got a cold too."

And so began a friendship that was to last all through our childhood, although we didn't know it then. We were just glad to have each other through the long days when we played, and told each other about home, and made up all manner of little stories that we acted out in great detail.

Then there were the nights when we cuddled together in one bed, whispering and giggling as the wind whistled around the old building and the trains moaned their way along the track, going who knew where. But although I already considered Shirley my very best friend, I never told her, or anybody else for that matter, about the dog who, every night without fail, spoke to me of Sly and home. Somehow, he was mine and mine alone.

Shirley was there about a week, and then I was alone again. They had finally decided that although it might not be the sole cause of my elevated temperature, my tonsils would have to come out. But nobody seemed to know just how such a thing would be accomplished.

Usually, one of the local ear-nose-and-throat doctors would come to the school and remove the tonsils of all the students who needed it. I can remember in later years how the smell of ether seemed to permeate that whole part of the campus on that day. The nurses only had time then for the most serious problems of those who weren't having the operation.

But at the time I needed to have my tonsils removed, all the local ENT specialists were in the Army, and nobody quite knew what to do. This was a common problem all over the country—the whole world really—but what did I care? I was stuck in that infirmary with a temperature that wouldn't go down, and Shirley was going downstairs, and I was being left behind.

"I brought you something," Fay said that night after supper when she came to visit.

"What?"

I didn't much care what it was unless she'd brought Shirley back, and even I knew she couldn't do that. But I thought it wouldn't be very polite not to at least pretend I was interested since she sounded so happy about it whatever it was.

"It's something Mama sent you, and something else I bought for you today. Which do you want first?"

"What you bought," I said. She bought the nicest presents, and I wonder now just how much of what was probably a small salary she spent on things she thought would make me happy, not to mention things, such as slippers, that I actually needed.

It was a toy telephone, complete with a dial that actually moved and returned to its original position with a realistic sound.

Now, I had never touched a telephone dial, had never actually talked on a telephone. Our house on the farm didn't boast of such a thing. Still, I knew all about telephones from listening to the radio, and this one sounded just like the ones on the radio did. Immediately I began to create little stories in which I would do all kinds of exciting things over the phone.

Patiently Fay taught me how to count from one to zero, identifying the numbers by the blank part of the dial, to the right of the one, and the stop next to the zero. She gave me numbers to dial and watched to see that I was doing it right. It would be years before the dial system came to our part of the country, but when it did, I was ready for it. Nobody had to teach me how to dial, thanks to Fay and that little telephone.

Then, I remembered.

"What did Mama send?" I asked as I told my imaginary telephone friend good-bye.

"Can you guess?" Fay asked, and I heard the rustle of paper.

I knew what I wanted more than anything, but because I

was afraid it wouldn't, couldn't, be, I said, "I can't guess. What is it?"

"Listen." And I heard Jane's little lamblike cry. Mama had sent Jane to keep me company, the thing I wanted the most in the whole world.

"It's Jane!" I cried, holding the doll close and smelling the faint odor of clothes dried in the sun and the wind. Mama had washed her bonnet and dress, bringing yet another part of home to me.

"It's time for me to go," Fay said, bending to kiss me. "Be a good girl, and don't cry."

"I won't," I promised, and tonight I wouldn't. I had so many things to tell Jane, and maybe if I tried really hard, I would be able to hear things from home that she knew.

At last it came, the day I'd been praying for. I was going downstairs.

"You'll have to come back to have your temperature checked," Miss Carson warned as she put Jane in my arms.

"Will I have to stay?"

Something in her tone made me afraid, and the day lost some of its joy.

"Well, we'll see," she said. "Maybe that temperature will behave itself when you get back with the other children."

So I had one glorious day of school, but I could tell by the way Miss Carson acted that afternoon that my temperature was probably up again. Suddenly my heart seemed heavy although it was pounding like the rain on the roof during a thunderstorm.

"Tomorrow's Saturday," Miss Carson said, and I heard the tinkle of the thermometer as she dropped it into the container of alcohol. "We'll see what happens then."

And the next day just before lunch—dinner as we called it—my worst fears were realized.

"I'm sorry, honey," Miss Carson said, "but it's still up. I hoped that maybe you were just worrying up here away from the other children. I thought maybe you'd get better if we tried you downstairs, but you haven't. Now, don't cry. I tell you what. You go on back down with your sister. And, Inez, you can bring her back after she has her dinner. Now, Inez, don't you cry too."

Not talking at all, an unusual thing for us, Nez and I left the infirmary, and she took me to Mrs. Keister. Nez's hand was almost as small as mine, and I felt it tremble as she squeezed my fingers.

"You go on upstairs and get ready for dinner, Inez," Mrs. Keister said. "Later, you can visit a little here in my room before you take Phyllis back to the infirmary. Go on, now. You come on, Phyllis, and wash your hands."

It was a raw, rainy day with a stiff wind that seemed to blow right through my coat as the line of little girls started along the porch to the dining room. I didn't want any dinner. It smelled like sauerkraut, and I didn't like sauerkraut. But I wouldn't have wanted any dinner even if it had been hot dogs, and I adored hot dogs with onions and lots of mustard, a treat for a little country girl in the 1940s. No, not even a big hot dog would have made me stop thinking about having to go back to the infirmary to stay.

It was just as I turned the corner from the Montague Hall porch to the one that led to the dining room that somebody picked me up and held me in a fierce, loving hug. It couldn't be, but somehow I knew it was—although I was almost afraid to hope, to even think it.

"Daddy?"

"How did you know?"

It was Mama's voice, and there she was, too, standing beside Daddy.

"I didn't mean to scare you," Daddy said, putting me down

and giving my little partner a hug too. "But when I saw my little girl, I couldn't help picking her up."

I heard Mrs. Keister's brisk steps coming along from the direction of the dining room, then heard her wonderful laugh, which somehow always seemed to express all the joy of living.

"Go on to dinner, Ellen," she said, giving my partner a pat. "This is Phyllis's mother and father."

I could hardly believe they were there even though they were holding my hands, one on either side of me.

"Mrs. French is sending Inez out," Mrs. Keister said as we started back toward Montague. "Does Fay know you're here?"

"We saw her when we first got here," Mama told her. "She'll be over as soon as she can leave work. I've talked to Mr. Healy, Phyllis, and we're going to take you home. They think you'll be fine as soon as you have your tonsils taken out, and Evelyn and Julian know a doctor in Lynchburg who can do it."

"Go home?"

I didn't want to go back to the infirmary, but I didn't want to go home, either. Well, not much. I hadn't even let myself think how much I missed Mama and Daddy until I'd seen them. But leave school? Leave Nez? Leave my teacher, and all those little dots that said things?

Then Mama said just the thing to make it bearable.

"I told Gray Boy and Sly that we might be bringing you back with us, and they're waiting."

It would be all right. I was going home, and my friends would be there waiting to greet me.

6

Visits from
the Sandman

The soul without imagination is what an observatory would be without a telescope.

HENRY WARD BEECHER

I didn't know the meaning of déjà vu, had never heard of it, not even on one of the radio soaps. Yet that was what I was experiencing on that Saturday morning in early September 1944. Once again I was sitting on the high stool in the infirmary, hearing the tinkle of the thermometer as Miss Carson dropped it back into the alcohol solution.

"I'm sorry," she was saying, "but you'll have to stay."

It was unreal, and as I sat there, listening to the monotonous sound of the deaf girls on the court below, I thought that I was dreaming. Soon, I'd wake up, and Mrs. Keister would be standing there, telling me to get up and brush my teeth.

Little prickles of hot, and then cold, ran from the back of my neck down to my legs and back up again. I tried to take a deep breath, and found that my heart was pounding so hard I couldn't do it. Then the tears came, big wet drops running down my nose and into my open mouth.

"I don't want to stay!" I wailed. "I won't stay!"

Already I was dreading that high cold bed, naptime, and grapefruit juice.

Mrs. Keister told me years later that when she turned on the light in the dormitory that morning, she had been unable to tell my face from the pillowcase, except for my mouth, which was a frightening red. She went straight for her thermometer, which registered an alarming one hundred and four degrees. She and Nez bundled me into my robe, and Mrs. Keister herself had gone with Nez and me to the infirmary.

"Here, here," Mrs. Keister said from beside my stool. She wiped my eyes with a handkerchief that smelled of peppermint. "That's not our big girl. Your nose is turning red."

I could hear what I now know were tears in her voice as she vainly tried to mop up the continuing flood.

I couldn't have cared less about my nose. I had had one week of school, and here I was again, only this time it was Saturday morning instead of Friday night like before.

It wasn't fair! I'd gone home the winter before and had had my tonsils taken out just the way Dr. Bradford had said I should. I had even stayed out for the rest of the school session. Now here I was again on that stool, and Miss Carson had said I would have to stay. A little worm of fear wiggled its way into my head as I wondered what I would have to have taken out this time.

Children of the 1940s knew little about such things as surgery, but I did know that if somebody from our little community went to the hospital for an operation, it was usually considered to be serious. I knew, too, that sometimes they died. I didn't want to die, but more than anything else, I didn't want to stay in the infirmary.

From the dining room downstairs came the sound of voices singing the morning blessing:

"Father, we thank You for the night, and for the pleasant morning light, for rest and food and loving care, for all that makes the world so fair. Amen."

As the last notes faded, there was a rush of sound as chairs were pulled out and dishes began to rattle.

"Inez, you're missing your breakfast," Miss Carson said. "I haven't ordered a tray for Phyllis, but her temperature is too high for her to eat, anyhow. How about some juice, miss?"

"What kind?" I asked around the lump in my throat. I was pretty sure I knew what the answer would be. In those days the school seemed to have only two kinds of canned juice—orange and grapefruit—and it was a toss-up as to which was more bitter.

"Grapefruit," she said with the same kind of enthusiasm in her voice that a gourmet would use when announcing a rare French wine.

I'd always been taught not to refuse anything to eat or drink when it was offered, but I'd had it with being polite that morning, and I didn't care if both Nez and Mrs. Keister were ashamed of me.

"No, thank you," I said.

"Maybe we can find some orange," Miss Carson said, and I heard her turn toward the infirmary kitchen across the hall,.

Well, that didn't do much for me, but then I remembered that she had said Nez wouldn't have any breakfast. I knew Nez didn't like that juice any more than I did, but I wanted her to have something. She always shared everything with me!

"Can Nez have some too?" I asked as I managed to make my way down off the stool.

"Don't you worry about her," Mrs. Keister said. "I'll find something for her, and she can eat in the little sewing room behind the practice room. You just think about getting well."

So it had started again—the lonely, hungry days and nights, the temperature that went up and down, and the tests. Things that I couldn't understand and that not even Dr. Bradford explained to me.

The only difference this time was that I wasn't quite as lonely. At the end of the first week, Fay Wine, the student helper who waited on the little girls' table, developed a cold. She wound up in the room with me for almost a week, telling me stories and spoiling me in every way she could.

Then, at the end of the second week, just as I was starting to miss Fay, a truly incredible thing happened. Nez was ushered in by Mrs. Lotts, and she got into the bed next to mine. She wasn't very sick. Her temperature seemed to be acting very much like mine, and though my trouble finally turned out to be caused by an unusual virus, they never quite determined what was wrong with Nez.

I didn't care. She was there, and my little world had changed for the better.

We whispered together during naptime. At night we played our usual little game of the Sandman who came on a white pony and told us all about all the wonderful places he had visited.

This was Nez's special story, and it seemed to fill that place of gloom with magic.

The white pony was particularly special to me, because one of the men in the community at home did indeed have a white pony. I had proudly had my picture taken on it the winter before when Lively had come home from the Service. To tell the truth, I'd been scared green, but Brother had said I wouldn't get hurt, so I'd let him "pose" me.

Later, of course, I forgot how scared I had been, and when

Nez invented the Sandman game, I felt like an expert on the subject of white ponies.

"You've got company, girls," Miss Carson said one Sunday afternoon.

Sister Fay usually came to see us at least once a day, but she was never announced.

"Who is it?" we asked almost together.

"Just guess," a voice said, and we surprised each other by bursting into tears. It was Mama, and where Mama was, Daddy was usually not far away.

They had come on other business, they told us. Daddy had decided to leave the farm, and he had come to see about a job at Western State Hospital, the state mental hospital for the western part of Virginia.

The summer before, Fay had left her job at the school switchboard to work at Western State in the business office, and she had told Daddy about the job in the power plant.

"But where will we live?" I asked.

"There's a nice house on the state farm," Fay said, "and we can rent it. I'll go on living on the hospital grounds where I live now, but I'll come home often, and I expect I'll be moving in with you soon."

Today, I marvel at how hard that decision must have been for Daddy. For as long as I could remember, he had always worked on the farm, renting the land. I'm sure that he knew there was no future for his family in such an arrangement, but still, the decision to leave the farm must have come hard. He was in his fifties, a time when we naturally resist change. Still, he willingly left a way of life he had always known, to find a better life for himself and for the rest of us.

It must have been a big decision for Mama too. I'm sure that the thought of a more convenient house must have been a bonus, yet, she, too, was leaving old friends and moving farther away from relatives. I truly believe, though, that she was contented just to be near her girls, and wherever Daddy went, she willingly followed.

Nez and I whispered a long time that night before the Sandman came for his usual visit. We wondered what our new home would be like. Fay and Mama and Daddy had done their best to describe it to us, but this is hard for somebody who can see to do for the blind. The only feature that truly struck our imagination was Fay's description of the circular staircase that went up from the reception hall.

I suspect that today's educators would have a stroke over my early reading habits. I can't remember when somebody wasn't reading to me, and because of my constant demands of, "read to me!" my family would have found it hard to read anything they wanted to read if they hadn't often simply read aloud whatever they were trying to read to themselves at the time. The result was that I became acquainted with many books that would be considered far too advanced for a child of my age. So I learned to know many characters that most children get to know at a much later age, and they were my friends long before I could read myself.

Little Women, Little Men, and even *Jane Eyre,* were all mixed in indiscriminately with Mother Goose rhymes and "Hansel and Gretel." Then there were my own personal delights, mysteries. My favorite authors were Carolyn Keene, creator of Nancy Drew, and Mary Roberts Rinehart.

One of our favorites, Nez's and mine, was Rinehart's *The Circular Staircase.* And now we were to have our very own circular staircase.

Mama and Daddy would be moving in about two months, and we could hardly wait to explore that staircase. Immediately we began to make plans to read the book while sitting on the steps.

There was just one problem in this, something that I hardly wanted to think about, and which I didn't even dare to ask about—the animals. Even I knew we would have to leave the cows, and Prince and Sam, the farm horses, and probably most of the chickens. But what about the cats? What about Sly? Not even the thought of our very own circular staircase completely banished the fear that they might be left behind.

"You girls are going home for a while," Mrs. Lotts said one Saturday afternoon about two weeks later as she rustled around the room, doing who knew what. You always read about nurses rustling in their starched uniforms, now a thing of the past since the coming of polyester and even pantsuits for nurses, but Mrs. Lotts really *did* rustle. Accompanying the rustle was a decided swish as her legs rubbed together. I don't exactly know what that was, because, since the onset of the war, nylon or even rayon stockings were almost impossible to get. At least, that was what Mama and Fay were always saying. But rustle and swish she did, and as she made her announcement, she seemed to be even more swishy and rustley.

"Going home?"

As usual we spoke in unison.

"But where's Mama?" This came from Nez.

"Your mother is in Mr. Healy's office."

There was disapproval in every syllable. I suppose Mrs. Lotts felt that it was an insult to her care, and it's possible somebody, probably Mama, had reminded her that the staff had been trying for about a month to diagnose the problem. But we, Nez and I, didn't care a whit. We were going home, where there would be plenty of good things to eat and drink, and where we could talk to our hearts' content.

"You'll have to go back as soon as you're better and the doctor says you can go," Mama warned Nez the next day. We'd both been examined by a doctor in Lynchburg, and I'd been given an injection of the new medicine called penicillin. "But Phyllis will stay home until next September," she continued. "Then Daddy and I will be close, and we can see to her."

So after a couple of weeks, Fay, along with her friend Kitty Chambers, came and took Nez back to school, leaving me with Mama and Daddy.

I wasn't lonely, though. Well, not much, because we were getting ready to move. Every day was filled with the plans that Mama always discussed with me as though I were a grownup, or at least as old as Nez.

"We can't take all the cats," she said. "I don't think it would be a good idea. They're good mousers, and several of the neighbors have said they'd like to have them. But we can take Gray Boy and Sly, of course."

So on a cold day in early November, I said good-bye to the first home I could remember. I said good-bye to the horses, and the cows, and the chickens, and to the last of the cats. I would miss them, of course, but my favorites—Gray Boy and Sly—were going with me.

Our cousins Charlie and Ora would take Mama and Daddy in their truck with the furniture and Gray Boy in the back. Safely nailed into a crate with air spaces, Gray Boy was one decidedly unhappy cat, but I thought he would understand when he got to his new home.

Fay, Sly, and I would be going in the car with Bill Dawson, who, in 1954, would marry Fay and offer Nez and me that rare and precious gift of a brother's love, even though there was no tie of blood.

As I heard the back-porch screen slam for the last time, I felt a strange mixture of sadness and anticipation. Although it was not a formulated thought, I knew that something never to be forgotten was coming to an end. At the same time, I sensed that many things waited, just waited for me to reach out and take them in my tiny hands.

Life, new and exciting, waited there on the other side of the Blue Ridge.

7

Buttons' World

*Animals are such agreeable friends; they ask no
questions, pass no criticisms.*

GEORGE ELIOT

Christmas is special, of course it is. Everybody knows that.
But for the pupils at the School for the Blind, it was *special!
special!*

For me, though, it is Christmas the year I was eleven that
stands out.

There was the usual excitement of name drawing and gift
exchange. There were parties, and, for the high school students, there was the long-planned-for, long-awaited Christmas
banquet. This feast was prepared and served by the members
of the home economics class under the direction of the
teacher, Mrs. Ann Culton, an indomitable lady who expected
the same hard work and dedication from her students, both

boys and girls, that she demanded from herself. And there was the Christmas program presented by the music department, featuring both the senior and junior choruses.

Today, I marvel at the quality of that music—difficult choral pieces, such as "The Carol of the Bells," "And The Glory of the Lord," as well as arrangements of carols. They would challenge an adult choir whose members could see the printed music, but were taken for granted as we memorized both music and words.

There were solos, too, both vocal and instrumental. I will never forget hearing Nez sing "Jesu Bambino," the high notes clear and true. I wondered deep inside my fanciful self if an angel had taken its place inside her for those brief moments. It is a long time since my eleven-year-old self wiped away the tears of joy for that beauty, but I still feel shivery when I remember how proud I felt on that night. That was *my* sister!

We younger girls didn't have the thrill of the high school banquet, not firsthand, that is. It was almost as thrilling for us to hear the big girls tell about it, though. I suppose it was a strange relationship, but it has always been something rare and beautiful. It was like sharing a world inhabited by about eighty brothers and sisters, but a world almost totally lacking in the usual sibling rivalry. Oh, we didn't always agree with one another. Some of our verbal battles would rival those on Capitol Hill for sheer ferocity! Still, we gloried in each other's good times, and cried when times were bad.

We felt no envy because the others who were older went to things we couldn't attend, and we enjoyed to the fullest their descriptions of the food and the candlelight, which most of us would never see with our physical eyes. We stroked the soft velvet of the winter dinner dresses and transformed the starched swish of our cotton school dresses into the rustle of taffeta. And we all wondered what it would be like to be going. Our time would come, though. Besides, we were going home for Christmas the next day, and nothing could be more wonderful than that.

I loved school, but there was no denying the joy of going home, and as I went skipping into the house that year, four days before Christmas, I wondered if anybody on earth was as happy as I was. Part of me wanted a doll for Christmas, and the rest of me wanted a cosmetics kit, complete with lipstick and nail polish. But nowhere in my wildest dreams was there even the notion of a puppy, a black cocker spaniel with floppy ears and curly fur.

We had moved from the house with the circular staircase after a year. Now we lived in the bottom half of a house right on the grounds of Western State Hospital, a location that never failed to win comments from our friends.

"Aren't you afraid to live there near all those crazy people?" or "I'd keep my doors locked and hide!" being among the mildest.

The truth is that we never thought of being afraid. Fay had carefully explained to Nez and me that those people were sick, just the same as if they had pneumonia or appendicitis. I have to confess that this kind explanation soon left my mind. To me, the patients were just ordinary people who acted funny. I accepted them as people, and we never shunned them.

In fact, it wasn't unusual for Mama and Fay to bring one of the women in so they could help her shorten a hemline, or so that they could give her a more presentable dress or a warmer coat from their own closet. And there is no telling how many goodies found their way from our kitchen into the hands of the patients.

The hospital, or the "asylum" as it was called in the beginning, opened its doors in 1829, ten years earlier than the Virginia School for the Deaf and Blind. Like the school, some of its buildings were designed with beauty in mind, but others were grim, functional structures that seemed to have simply been dropped there, with no apparent aim at arrangement.

The grounds were beautiful, though, with huge old trees and grass that was soft and springy under my feet. The current hospital is made up of well-planned modern buildings, located near our first home in the Staunton area (the house of the circular staircase), and the original hospital is now the Staunton Correctional Center. The new hospital is modern and not at all grim, but I find it a shame that those spacious lawns couldn't have been taken along with the people.

Of course, the most disturbed patients were, and still are, confined on locked wards. They were exercised regularly, though, when the weather permitted, walking in long lines with attendants strategically placed along the line. I can still hear the slow shuffle of their feet along the gravel road, and the hum of their voices, murmuring who knew what—wisdom or folly. But many were allowed to move freely around the grounds, pursuing their own affairs, whether they were real or the creations of their own secret fears or longings.

So, on that Friday afternoon as Nez and I came home for the Christmas vacation, we weren't the least bit surprised to hear Daddy at the back door sharing Mama's Christmas cookies with Joe Clark, one of the "outside" patients. Joe had made something of a reputation for himself by building sturdy pens and collecting every stray dog he could find.

"Thank Mrs. Staton for me," he was saying. "I've got to go feed my dogs."

We could hear his feet on the brittle winter grass. Then, to our surprise, he stopped, and abandoning his usual mumble, he said, "Good Lord, Mr. Staton! What's that thing your son's got?"

At that, Mama must have done the world's fastest about-face, because we heard her open the front door, which she'd just closed after letting us in. Nez and I rushed to follow her back onto the front porch. Although her language wasn't the same as Joe's, her tone certainly was almost identical.

"Lively, what's that?"

And as though in answer to both questions, we heard "*woof woof!*" moving up the walk toward us.

"Isn't he cute?" Lively said. I noticed that he seemed to be speaking a bit more heartily than usual, no doubt a show of bravado.

"Who does he belong to?" This from Daddy, who dearly loved dogs and who had probably missed our old Sly more than any of us knew.

Sly had been an old dog when we moved from the farm, and he had died before we left the house of the circular staircase. He had apparently followed Daddy to work one day, and although Daddy and Lively had looked, we never knew what had happened to him. I had quietly cried myself to sleep for weeks. Even today, when I know that country-bred animals often seek solitude for death, I feel little prickles of tears when I think about that good, faithful hound.

"No more dogs!" Mama had decreed when it became apparent that Sly would never come home. But there we stood on that December day, with the wind blowing the bare branches, and Lively was saying:

"He's got his papers and everything. Here, Phyl, look at him. He's black. Feel his ears. Here he is, Nez. Isn't he cute!"

"Well, he is cute," Mama conceded, "but who does he belong to?" I think in her hearts of hearts she knew. Lively had missed old Sly too.

"He belonged to the girl whose father owns the Dog House. She lives in a trailer, and—"

"Owns the what?" Mama really sounded confused.

"You know, Mama. That place that sells the foot-long hot dogs. Anyhow, she lives in a trailer, and he chewed up almost all her clothes, and she wanted to get rid of him, and—"

"And you brought him home to chew up all our clothes."

"Oh, he won't do that, Mama," Lively protested. "He was just lonesome by himself all day. He's just a puppy. We can teach him to be good."

"Who can teach him?" Mama asked, but somehow I had the feeling she just might be weakening.

"I will," he said, and even I knew he wouldn't. But I wanted that puppy.

"I've even got him some food," Lively went on, and I heard the rustle of a bag.

"What's that?" Mama asked.

"Dog food, Mama."

"I can see that. But what kind of dog would want that stuff?"

I heard her give a sniff, but she didn't say anything else on that particular subject. Instead, she attacked from another direction.

"Where's he going to sleep?"

"On the back porch," Lively said, guiding my hand to the little stub of a tail, which was in perpetual motion as though that dog's fate wasn't being discussed right there in front of him.

"Oh, all right." Mama gave in. "I don't suppose he'll get cold, but we'll all freeze standing out here talking."

Early the next morning I heard Mama's soft voice coming from the kitchen. I opened the bedroom door as quietly as I could and stuck my head out to listen.

"Imagine expecting a dog to eat that dry stuff!" she was saying, and since I didn't hear anything except a pant, I assumed she was talking to the dog, whose name, Lively had told us, was Buttons.

"Come on, boy, do you like bacon? I'll go to the store today and get you some real dog food. If you're going to live here, you're not going to starve."

So that was that. Buttons became a part of the family, waiting for his share of tidbits in the kitchen, and sleeping wherever he chose in the house, and finding a place in the heart of everybody in the family, especially Mama's. Did Lively deliberately buy the cheapest, most repulsive dog food in the store, knowing the one thing that would spark Mama's pity and then her love? Well, of course he did!

It wasn't long before Buttons discovered that the world held a lot more than what was to be found in his own house. Today much is said about pet therapy for children, seniors, and the mentally ill, but good old Buttons found it out all by himself.

They loved him, those lonely souls, many of them either without any family, or with family who, after leaving them in a mental hospital, considered them as dead. Buttons didn't know or care that they talked to themselves or to those seen only by them. They patted him, told him how handsome he was, and gave him all manner of food.

I'm surprised that it took six months for him to get into trouble, but it was late June when the security guard from the hospital showed up at our front door for the first time.

"Is this your dog?" he asked. Actually, there was no need to ask, because Buttons had run through the open door, straight to the living room where he flopped down on a rug and began to lick his paws.

"Yes, it is," Mama said, no doubt wondering what new embarrassment Buttons was about to inflict on her. The week before, he had quietly followed her downtown, to emerge suddenly from behind her at Wilson's drugstore. Mr. Wilson and everybody else thought it was funny. Mama wasn't amused, though. She had tried vainly to pretend Buttons didn't belong to her, although she had taken great pains to see that he got home safely. Now here was the hospital security guard bringing him home.

"He was making himself at home on a patient's bed. Now,

Mrs. Staton, we can't have that. It's against the rules, you understand. Keep him home for a few days, won't you?"

We fastened Buttons' chain to the clothesline, where he huddled in misery for the prescribed few days. The instant we let him go, off he went again to find his friends, no doubt to hear what had been happening on the wards during his enforced absence.

And they were his friends. Men and women, young and old, they loved him. All except one, and that one exception was that rescuer of stray dogs, Joe Clark.

I know nothing of Joe's life before he became a part of the hospital community. Mr. Word, the superintendent of buildings and grounds, did tell us that Joe had been there for years. It was the only home he could remember for a long time, or perhaps ever. The illness that brought patients to the hospital often obliterated the memory of the life and home they left behind. Considering Joe's love for dogs, his feelings toward Buttons seemed strange, but after one conversation with him on the subject, all was clear. Joe loved dogs, but for some unknown reason he loved mixed breeds, and Buttons was a purebred.

"I don't like them kinds of dogs," he told Daddy, and Buttons, with that rare gift of understanding which many animals have, never imposed himself on Joe.

We are often told that it is a mistake to attribute to animals the kind of understanding that humans possess, but in saying that, I'm not doing so. That dog and many other animals I've known well have possessed a tolerance and understanding that many people lack.

Today, of course, the treatment of mental illness is vastly different from what it was in the 1940s. Even today, though, many people shun the mentally ill, as if their suffering were contagious, or something that could be controlled if the patient "just had enough willpower."

Modern drugs and other treatments have dramatically increased the chances for a complete cure. Along with public enlightenment, they have made the lot of the mentally ill vastly different from those days. But now as then, a good, loving animal can often make a big difference.

"Something's happening up the road toward the dump," Mama called from the bedroom window early one morning. It was just before school started that next September. "I see two of the doctors and a lot of other people heading that way."

We were all pretty sure what it was that would bring a medical team to that part of the grounds. The staff was vigilant, but those bent on suicide usually found a way, and the big trees along that road afforded a handy means, along with a piece of rope or string, or even the patient's own belt.

It was sad, but it was something that happened, and even I came to understand that the terrific suffering that had led the man or woman to such a tragic final act had come to an end. He or she was in the hands of a merciful, loving God.

"Mr. Staton! Mr. Staton!"

It was Joe calling from the backyard.

"Somebody's hung himself, and that dog of yours is up there sitting by him. They ain't cut him down yet."

"Oh, my Lord," Mama said. "Oscar, for goodness sake, go get him."

"Let me go where I can see better," Daddy said. "Maybe Joe's wrong."

But Joe was seldom wrong, and he wasn't wrong that time, either.

There Buttons sat, right in the midst of the investigative team while they were making their notes and whatever else it was that they did at such a time.

"He came along when I put his leash on," Daddy said as he patted a Buttons strangely lacking his usual enthusiasm at seeing us, even if he had just been in the backyard for five minutes.

"Did anybody say anything?" Mama asked, no doubt thinking about his previous excursions to the wards.

"Dr. Fulton said good morning," Daddy reported, "but nobody said a word about Buttons. I just put his leash on, and we came home. Banner, he was sitting there like he was guarding that poor man, and I couldn't help thinking that maybe he felt more—well, love for that poor old soul than any of us there."

So, Buttons, that bundle of mischief and love, had kept a final vigil beside a friend before impersonal hands took over, performed the necessary tasks, and took him to his final rest.

8

Superintendent Robin

*Endurance is the crowning quality and patience all
the passion of great hearts.*

JAMES RUSSELL LOWELL

Robin was a collie, big and soft, with floppy ears that
invited you to flip them back and forth. His tail would have
served admirably as a lady's fan in the gracious parlors of the
Southern mansions, because it seemed never to stop moving,
gently stirring the air around it.

Where Buttons was a curly package of rollicking mischief,
Robin moved sedately through the days, seemingly surrounded
by an aura of love and patience. And surely no animal who ever
lived needed both love and patience more than that big collie.

Probably he often found himself thinking, "Children, children everywhere, and not a place to hide!" And there was a
lot of truth in that. In those days, the total enrollment at the

school, counting both the deaf and the blind, was around four hundred, and just about everybody in both departments wanted to pet or tease Robin.

The deaf children must have been the most confusing for him, for they usually couldn't communicate with him verbally. Because of this, they often did things to see the results. Unfortunately, in many cases these things amounted to teasing. When he was young, at least, he would simply melt into the crowd and seek the gentler company of the blind children.

But there were pitfalls there too. There was a lot of Robin, especially that fan of a tail, and if he let down his guard, he was liable to have some part of his anatomy stepped on. As he grew older, he showed his disapproval of the teasing, but in all his long life, I never knew him to so much as yelp when a blind child stepped on him. Instead, he would push the offender gently with his head, and give her a lick, as if to say, "You're on my paw, but it's okay if you'll just move, please."

No White House pet ever attended more functions than Robin. He belonged to Mr. Healy, the superintendent, and at first, wherever his master went, he went. Then, as he passed from puppyhood into the more sophisticated world of a mature dog, he began going places on his own. Everything from wrestling matches to the Christmas concert was held with Robin looking on, adding his stamp of approval.

The concerts were the most hazardous. In those days, no concert or graduation ceremony was held without music from the school orchestra, dubbed the Dishpan Symphony by the students. I don't suppose it was actually that bad, but it can't be denied that sometimes it did produce a clatter and squeak that might not be considered exactly harmonious. More than one of us disgraced ourselves by giggling in the middle of "Pomp and Circumstance," or a solemn introduction to the school song, when somebody in the brass section lost control of his instrument.

But that was nothing compared to the uproar caused when Robin was in the audience. After a while, of course, we became accustomed to his accompaniment, but for the first few times we were almost in hysterics no matter how serious the occasion.

I say "accompaniment," but, in truth, I suppose that the music hurt his ears. Still, it sounded for all the world as though he was howling in time with the music. Actually, he was polite about the whole thing, going out of the chapel and standing outside the door, where he flung back his head, and as Ray Houser, one of the big boys, said, "Let 'er fly."

Not only did Robin attend every school function, but he visited the kitchen, the classrooms, the dormitories, and even offered love and encouragement to the patients in the infirmary. In short, he seemed to feel that every part of the school community was his responsibility.

There was, however, one big problem for Superintendent Robin, as we sometimes called him, and that was the summer vacation. I imagine that he was completely baffled by the abrupt disappearance of all his charges. One minute they were there; then, within the space of a few hours, the place was quiet and empty. Of course, the dietician, Mrs. Houff— Little Mary Lillian, as she called herself—was there, and he could still expect to hear her honeyed tones calling, "Come on, little Robin, and get your little breakfast." With Little Mary Lillian, everything and everybody was little.

Despite this, poor Robin must have been lost during the summer vacation. I have a feeling he would even have welcomed a few big deaf boys to pull his tail.

To be honest, many of us were almost as bad as Robin. We counted the days until the close of school, when our mothers would pack our trunks and we'd go home for the summer. There were the tearful good-byes with our friends, followed by the laughing reunions with our family, and then....

Suddenly our whole routine had changed, and although it was a luxury not to have to get out of bed at six A.M. and get ready for a rather tasteless breakfast, it was different. Before long, we found ourselves thinking about September, although, of course, our feelings were mixed. We loved our family and home and animals, but somehow our thoughts kept going to the school, our friends and teachers—and Robin. And for me there was the added sorrow of missing my music lessons.

I was in the fifth grade when Mama took the money she had been saving to buy a washing machine and bought a secondhand piano. It was an old upright with a stool that whirled deliciously as I adjusted the height. Not much of a piano, I'm afraid, but no owner of a Steinway grand could have been happier than Nez and I were. Now I could play, and we could sing to our hearts' content.

We were still living on the hospital grounds, and I realize now that the patients probably found comfort and joy in listening. As for the family, I suspect we just about drove them mad as we practiced old hymns, popular tunes, and—ambition of ambitions—Malotte's "The Lord's Prayer," which taxed the ability of my little hands but which Nez's clear, true voice mastered with ease.

"Miss Lena is going to give you piano lessons this summer," Mama told me that year soon after we had gone home for the vacation.

Second only to Nez, Miss Lena was my idol. If I could just grow up to be like Miss Lena, I'd ask for nothing else. I was convinced that if Nez or Miss Lena couldn't do a thing, it couldn't be done by any blind person who had ever lived.

Miss Lena had come to the school as a young child, and after graduating, she had stayed on to work, first as housemother to the little girls, and then to teach basketry and music. She was my music teacher during the school year, and now, thanks to the new piano at home, I could take lessons during the summer.

As far as I know, Miss Lena didn't have any near relatives, and she lived at the school winter and summer. To us girls, her room on the second floor of Montague Hall was something special. A girl could always find a welcome there, and many little secrets and woes were entrusted to her sympathetic ears. Miss Lena would sit in her little sewing rocker, her knitting needles clicking as her visitor sat usually on her cedar chest. Somehow, after a talk there in that peaceful place, the world seemed kinder, or at least not so frightening.

There were good times there too. In those days almost nobody had heard of television, and radio was the thing. For young people today, the radio is something that provides music, news, and weather reports, a background noise. In those days, however, it was a major form of entertainment, and Miss Lena welcomed us to listen to her radio, especially the afternoon stories.

Often I'm tempted to buy a series of the old radio soap operas, but I must admit that I'm afraid to. Perhaps they would seem trite and unrealistic, and I cherish my memories of afternoons filled with excitement and anticipation, sitting there on Miss Lena's cedar chest or on the rug in front of her chair, listening to "When a Girl Marries," "Portia Faces Life," "Backstage Wife," and others whose names have gone the way of many other youthful memories.

Those characters and events were real to all of us, including Miss Lena.

I remember once when we were sure one of the characters in "When a Girl Marries" was going to be convicted of murder. Just as the jury was about to come in, Miss Lena suddenly rushed to the door.

"I can't stand to listen, girls!" she cried out in a strangled-sounding voice. "You listen and tell me what the verdict is."

So it was with an absolute thrill of joy that I heard I would be taking piano lessons with Miss Lena that summer. And we would have a chance to discuss our favorite characters too! I saw Miss Lena years later, after she had gone to live in a nursing home, and I was delighted to find that she had never lost that strange combination of dignity and youthful enthusiasm. Those qualities had made her someone to be looked up to and a companion on our own level, all at the same time.

Twice a week that summer Mama and I would walk the eight or so blocks to the school, where I would pound away at the old upright in Miss Lena's combination basketry room and music studio. Sometimes Mama would go to town to shop, and when I finished my lesson, Miss Lena and I would go over to Montague. We would sit in big rockers on the porch that ran across the front of the building while we waited for Mama to come back.

It was there one afternoon, soon after I'd started my lessons, that Robin found us. With an uncharacteristic yelp of joy, he threw himself at me, licking my hands and then my face. Then, remembering his manners, he gave his other friend, Miss Lena, a polite greeting, only to run back to me.

It was a hot day, and when Mama returned, a little later than usual, she brought us a treat—a Pepsi for me and orangeade for herself and Miss Lena.

As we sat there on the shady porch sipping our drinks, Mama and Miss Lena talked about Lively's recent marriage. Grace was a tiny thing, hardly as tall as my five feet. I had already told Miss Lena how small she was and how motherly her voice sounded. Now Mama told her about their apartment, which was downtown, right across the street from the police station.

Then Miss Lena told us about a frightening experience she had a couple of days earlier.

As usual during the summer, she was the only person living in Montague. Now, nobody could ever deny that that building was what might be called eerie at night when filled with people. But when empty except for yourself, it must have been positively frightening. Like most old buildings, it had its share of ghosts, folks who had died there and who just might return to walk where they had walked in life—although nobody could say just why they would want to do such a thing. And, of course, there was the chapel. During the Civil War it had been a hospital, the scene of who knew what suffering. Did those souls leave their lonely, often unmarked graves to wander the area where they had spent their last minutes of life?

I didn't know what Miss Lena's private fantasies were, but since these were mine, I could imagine how she must have felt several nights earlier when she sensed something moving quietly along beside her as she went down the hall from her room to the bathroom.

"Nobody knows how hard it was for me to come back to my room," she said, "but I couldn't stay there in the bathroom all night. I opened the door—and there it was. I couldn't exactly hear it, but I knew it was there, right beside me."

"What did you do?"

I was almost beside myself. This was better than Nancy Drew.

"I went back to my room," she said, "and I didn't tell anybody the next day. The next night, though, it happened again. I told myself that if anybody was there, Mr. Ham would see them. After all, he's been the night watchman here for over thirty years, and he knows his business. But it would be easy for someone to hide when he made his rounds."

Real easy if it was a ghost, I thought.

"But the next day I thought I'd better say something. When Mabel came to clean the bathroom, I told her, and she began to look around. And what do you suppose she found?"

"I wouldn't have any idea!" Even Mama sounded excited.

"A mother cat and four kittens," Miss Lena said, apparently pleased with the effect of her story. "She had made a nest in one of the dormitory rooms, and they're still there. They aren't bothering a soul, and now that I know the thing following me is just a cat, I don't care."

But I knew even then what a relief it must have been to discover what that stealthy thing was.

All that talk about Lively's apartment and Miss Lena's cat was exciting for us, but it put Robin to sleep. He was still napping when Mama and I left to walk home, and we didn't disturb him.

The next day was one of those summer days that feels more like September and that makes you want to cling to the warmth of your bed as long as possible. Nez and I had settled back for just a little longer when we heard Daddy call us.

"Get up, girls. You've got company."

And there on the front porch stood Robin, wagging from one end to the other. Mama was sure he hadn't followed us home, and to this day, I'm not sure how he found us. A call to Mr. Healy brought over Mr. Cason, who worked in school maintenance and always collected the school's mail. That day, he collected Robin too. But the next morning, there Robin was again. Again, Mr. Cason collected him on his way to the post office. And, again, the next morning—there was Robin!

Finally, everybody except Robin gave up, and he was a familiar sight all that summer. Like any good houseguest, he would visit for a while, then go home, negotiating the streets with care.

On several occasions we had a reason to visit the school, coming home after dark. As we left the campus, there was Robin, appearing apparently from nowhere. He would walk with us as far as our front walk, where Mama said he would stand watching, like the gentleman he was, until we'd gone in the house. Then he would make his way back to the school and the superintendent's residence. At first, we had been worried, and we had called Mr. Healy to make sure Robin had made it home safely. Robin was always there, enjoying his favorite rug.

Robin had found his friends, and Nez and I had found an added time of fun in our summer vacation.

9

Rainbow Dreams

The future is always a fairyland to the young.

GEORGE AUGUSTUS SALA

And so the years moved along, taking me with them, changing the child into the woman, molding, and shaping.

There were changes at the school too. Our Mrs. Keister retired and went to live with her niece, Virginia, and her husband, John. But since Ginny and John lived in Staunton, she and Ginny were frequent visitors at the school.

Montague, with its hissing radiators and things that scurried overhead in the night, was left to itself, and the girls occupied Battle Hall, a modern building with its own kitchen and dining room.

It seemed only weeks ago that I had come to the school for the first time, so full of dreams and hopes and fears. And now, though it hardly seemed at all possible, I was about to leave.

The holidays, the last I would spend as a pupil at the Virginia school, came with a bound that year. One minute it was September, and I was filled with the excitement of leaving home and settling in at the school for my senior year; the next, it was December, and I was stepping off the Trailways bus and Fay was hugging me to the sound of bell ringers from the Salvation Army.

In 1954, Fay had married Bill Dawson, the same Bill who had driven us to our new home, the house of the circular staircase, so many years earlier. A former forest ranger, Bill possessed the quiet warmth that is a special quality acquired by those who have lived alone with nature. His voice was deep, and his hands were strong and gentle. In his presence, you could imagine that world of wild creatures, clear streams, and trees mature when Native Americans roamed free through the forests. They complemented each other—Bill, with his dignity and love of music and living things, and Fay, with her ability to turn any gathering into a special party and her flair for transforming the most dismal room into a place of elegance and style on the smallest of budgets.

With two such parents, it wasn't surprising that Pam, who was almost four, was a sensitive, loving child.

Four months after Pam's birth, Mama, that gentle presence, died. Her great joy had been that she had lived to see her grandchild, hold her, and whisper words of love.

Two years before Mama's death, Daddy had suffered a stroke that left him nearly helpless. Although I'm sure Mama regretted leaving all of us, I'm sure that leaving Daddy must have been her greatest sorrow.

"As long as I've got a home, you've got a home," Bill told me the day I learned that Mama had cancer. "There's my house up in the country. Fay and I are going to give up our apartment, and we'll stay with you until your mama's gone.

We'll move up home then, and you and Nez and Oscar will go with us."

That had been in February, and on April twenty-seventh, her birthday, Mama died. In May we all left Lynchburg, where we had lived since Fay and Bill were married, and headed for the little community of Agricola. We moved into the old farmhouse that had been built by Bill's grandfather, and weekdays Bill drove into nearby Lynchburg to work.

And now here I was, more than three years later, coming home for my last high school Christmas break. I hugged Fay and kissed Pam. Then I hugged and kissed them all over again.

"Nez is coming soon, soon, soon," Pam sang to the tune of "Jingle Bells." "Can I have some money for the kettle, please?"

"When will she be here?" I asked, as I handed her the loose change from my wallet.

"Your bus was a local," Fay explained. "She'll be coming from Richmond on an express. It should be here any minute."

Nez was taking training evaluation at what was then called the Virginia Commission for the Blind. Now it's the Virginia Department for the Visually Handicapped.

It would be quite a houseful. There were Daddy and his brother, Uncle Lonie, who also lived with Fay and Bill and helped Fay with Daddy. Then there were Fay, Bill, and Pam, Nez and me, and Porter, the elderly black man who had come to live with Bill's parents when he was a young boy. And although the house was well off the main road, somebody was always dropping in to sit by the fire, talk, and, of course, eat. Poor Fay! I don't know how she did it, but she looked after us—all of us. She made clothes for Nez, Pam, and me. She nursed Daddy. And she cooked and baked and loved everybody.

"What's Santa Claus going to bring?" I asked Pam that night as we sat in the kitchen, waiting for the first pan of Christmas cookies to come out of the oven. Outside, the wind whistled around the house, rattling the windows as though trying to force its way in, but here in the kitchen, it was cozy and warm. The house smelled of chocolate and spices and—best of all!—the sharp, prickly smell of the cedar tree Bill's nephews Harry and Buddy had cut late that afternoon from Bill and Fay's own woods.

"Santa is going to bring me a kitten," Pam announced with the assurance of a three-year-old who knows she'll soon be four.

"Now, Pam," Fay said. She set a pan of cookies on the counter with a thump. "You know Santa isn't going to bring you a kitten."

"Then I'll get it for my birthday. You know my birthday is Christmas Day." Pam snuggled on my lap to impart that bit of information.

"We know that, Pam," Fay said, popping a cookie into my mouth, "but you aren't going to get a kitten."

"Well, maybe it'll be a cat, but that's what I'm going to get."

"But you have Half Pint," I reminded her, hoping to avoid a Christmas crisis. Bill very definitely—according to him, at least—did not like cats. Half Pint was a rather elderly beagle who had lived there for years, even before the death of Bill's parents. He was a dear old boy, reminding me of our old Sly, but, as Pam put it in no uncertain terms:

"Well, yes. But, Phyl, he isn't a cat."

Later, after we had tucked Pam in for the night and returned to the kitchen, I asked Fay, "What on earth put it into her head that she's going to get a cat for Christmas?"

"I haven't the slightest idea," she said, and I heard the lid on the cookie jar give its usual little rattle. "She'll forget it."

That was four days before Christmas, but as the day drew closer, Pam seemed to become even more sure that she was going to get a cat.

"Maybe next spring we'll get a kitten," Bill said finally. "This isn't the time of the year for kittens. They'd get cold."

"But it could stay in the house where it's warm."

"What makes you so sure you're going to get a kitty for Christmas, honey?" I asked her the evening before Christmas Eve.

"I just know."

She was standing at her bedroom window, apparently looking out at the winter evening.

"I see the sunset, Phyl," she said. "It's. . . it's—oh, it's so pretty! Phyl, I wish you could see it. I wish I knew how to tell you what it looks like. Oh, Phyl, it's so pretty!"

I could hear tears in that child's voice, tears for what I couldn't see. They were tears of real sorrow, because there was no way she could share with me the beauty she saw. For a moment, I felt the pressure of my own unshed tears—not for myself, but for her—and I found myself almost praying for her to have that cat.

Nez and Fay came into the room from upstairs where they had been discussing some deep holiday secret, and the spell was broken. The wind rattled the back door, and Half Pint sent his hunting cry over the cold landscape, and I wiped my eyes.

The next day was windy, with little rattles of sleet on and off all day.

Bill's brother, Dick, and his wife, Jo, always invited the Dawson family to supper on Christmas Eve to help them celebrate their wedding anniversary. Fay fixed an early supper for Daddy, Uncle Lonie, and Porter, who lived together in a cabin not far from the main house. Nez and I were going to have a frozen pizza while we listened to a recording of Dickens's *A Christmas Carol.*

"Now, remember—you'll find your pizza on the top shelf of the freezer when you're ready to put it in the oven," Fay said, and I heard her putting the dishes on the tray for the men. "I'll take this down and save Uncle Lonie a trip. It's turning cold, and—"

I have no idea what the rest of the sentence was going to be, because all of a sudden she set the tray down with a clatter and jingle.

"What's wrong?"

She was standing at the sink where she could see out of the big kitchen window, and I felt sure she had seen something that had startled her.

"It's—"

"It's my cat coming down the road!" Pam squealed. She jumped up and down, making the dishes in the cabinets rattle. "It's my cat! Nez, Phyl, it's my cat! It's my gray cat! Mama, it's my cat!"

The rest of us just stood there. Then, as though to confirm what Pam had said, I heard a meow. It was a cat, all right.

"Where did that cat come from?" Bill almost blew through the back door. "Don't tell me. Santa brought it."

"Well, yes, Daddy."

"It looks like a stray," Fay told us later after she had fed it and fixed it—no, her—a place to sleep. "We're over a mile off the main road. Where on earth did it come from?"

"Santa brought her," I ventured, and was rewarded with a thrown cookie, which landed in my mouth.

We never did discover where she, Tinker Belle—Pam's choice of names, my spelling—came from. But there she was, and there she stayed.

Maybe. . . just maybe? Could Bill have been right? Who really knows for sure when a child wishes, especially at Christmas. . . .

The rest of that school year sped by on silken paws.

That year marked the first time the students were taught cane-travel, now grandly called "orientation and mobility."

"I'm expected to walk with that thing!" I complained as the instructor, Dan Meisenheimer, put the cane, a long fiber-glass contraption, in my hand. "I'll look like a blind woman walking around with a white cane."

Well, I knew how silly that sounded, but I said it, anyway.

"It's not white," he said. "It's silver, and you *are* blind."

And we were both laughing. Dan was a special, consider-ate person who drove an incredibly small sports car and weighed almost three hundred pounds.

The cane is moved in an arc roughly the distance from shoulder to shoulder, going to the left as the right foot steps forward and to the right as the left foot moves. Thus the path is explored before the foot moves. It is safe and efficient if you do it right, but we were just learning. One careless move, one lapse of attention, and accidents can and do happen.

If I said that I, and probably everybody else in the class, wasn't scared green, I'd be fibbing. There were all sorts of hazards out there—dogs, traffic, trash cans, and people who stood there in your path just to see what you would do. But with all this, I don't think that anybody ever had a serious accident. Dan Meisenheimer was always there, watching and encouraging us.

"Today we're going to do something different," he announced one windy day in March. "I've pointed out all the landmarks, the way the building lines are arranged, unusual dips in the sidewalk, all those things we've talked about. Now, today, I'm going to take you two at a time in the car and let you out. I won't tell you where you are, but I'll meet you at Quick's in half an hour. The length of time is longer than necessary, so I can come back and get a couple more people. I know that every chance you get you haunt Quick's to eat hamburgers, so you won't mind."

I thought it would be a breeze. All I had to do was follow the route, paying attention to the turns the car made. But, what with the rather strange turns and Dan Meisenheimer's constant conversation, I was completely lost.

My partner that day was Danny Dyer, another senior.

"Don't worry," Danny said as the putt-putt of the little car disappeared. "It's easy. I know which direction the wind is coming from. It's a piece of cake!"

It should have been. Unfortunately, what we didn't know was that while we were in the car, the wind had changed.

I don't know how long we would have roamed around in what we thought was the right direction if the town clock hadn't bonged loudly, announcing that it was ten o'clock, and giving us our bearings. After that, it *was* a piece of cake. Well, almost.

"I hope you aren't like the rest of them," Mr. Hickman, my English teacher, said one morning in April, a few weeks later.

"Sir?"

"Tomorrow is the closing day for the conservation contest, and nobody has written an essay, though everyone promised. You know our school is competing with all the other high schools in the state. I'd like to have at least one entry."

My heart almost stopped. What with term papers, cane-travel, the coming spring recital, and everything else, the essay contest had completely slipped my mind. How on earth could I tell him?

"Tomorrow?" I said trying to think of an excuse and knowing there wasn't one.

"That's right. Do you have it finished?"

"I haven't typed it."

That was the gospel truth.

"That's all right. You can type it during English period tomorrow." There was relief in his voice.

What was I going to do? It really wasn't that I was afraid of the consequences. The essay contest had nothing to do with our regular English class and wouldn't affect my grade one way or the other. No, it was the thought that he would be disappointed—and disappointed in me.

The answer was simple. I'd have to write something. So that night, after everybody was in bed, I sat on the edge of the bathtub so I wouldn't disturb my roommates and worked on the short essay I'd started after supper.

At midnight I finished, and breathed a prayer of thanks that the required length had been short—only seven hundred and fifty words.

The next day I typed the wretched thing, turned it in, and forgot about it. Then one day a month or so later, I met Mrs. Davis, who had been my fourth-grade teacher, as we were both going to lunch.

"I'm so proud of you, Phyllis!" she gushed, giving me a hug. "Your teachers are all proud of you. I always told your mother that you were going to be a writer, remember? I do wish she was here."

Yes, I remembered that she had always said I was going to be a writer, but what was she talking about? Then I recalled the contest. Surely I hadn't won anything. If I had, I didn't deserve it. I could have worked harder.

I'd just opened my mouth to ask Mrs. Davis what she was talking about when she called to another teacher and I heard her rushing across the driveway.

Later, in civics class, Mr. Tyler, my homeroom teacher, told me that I had won an honorable mention. It is true that I worked hard to finish that essay, but to this day, I've never felt true pride in the accomplishment.

The year moved on, with its triumphs, large and small, and its events, bittersweet and memorable.

Soon it was late May. Graduation loomed ahead, and we were moving toward the senior dance, which was something of a social event for the entire high school. My date was Bob

Rinker. Bob had graduated ahead of me and was now back as an assistant to Mr. Cronise, who taught piano tuning.

The theme, a popular one that we were repeating from another year, was "Somewhere Over the Rainbow," and Jeanine Ford, a sophomore, was going to sing the theme song, "Over the Rainbow."

"Will you play for me, please, Phyllis?" she asked. "I know that it's your special dance, and maybe it isn't fair to ask you to work, but it would mean a lot to me."

How could she know how much it would mean to me to be able to take part for this one last time?

My dress for that dance was a pale yellow.

"You'll have to have talisman roses to go with that dress," Mrs. Bowman, who taught sewing, told me. She supervised our dresses and flowers and just about anything else to do with style.

"But where will we put it?" I giggled, feeling the skimpy top.

"You'll have a wrist corsage," she said.

"But I'm playing," I protested.

"They'll have to make it for the left wrist, and be sure it fits. River Hill Gardens, the flower shop in Churchville, is doing the flowers. Mr. Campbell is a true artist. I'll talk to him."

So a few evenings later, I sat and played for the last time in the old chapel. As Jeanine sang of that magic land where bluebirds fly and dreams come true, I smelled the delicate roses at my wrist.

And for a brief moment, that land of the song became mine—a world of hope and of promise where anything was possible, the magical land of my future.

10

Life's Little Miracles

No one ever gets far unless he accomplishes the impossible at least once a day.

ELBERT HUBBARD

It was a night of magic, or so it seemed to me as I stood there at the head of the flight of steps that led to the backyard. More than thirty years have passed since then, yet I can still feel it, that sense of wonder and promise, the joy of living, in one quiet nocturnal space of time.

That I couldn't physically see the moon or the night sky made no difference. I knew they were there. I knew it with the same certainty that I knew of the existence of their Creator, Who can't be seen with the physical eye.

The three-quarter moon was the silver pin I could remember at the neck of Mama's dress. The stars were hard, cold points of ice on the water bucket back in that long-ago life on the farm. The night sky was the soft velvet lining of the jewelry box I'd been given for my twelfth birthday—soft and dense and somehow mysterious.

But I saw so much more in that night of magic. There was the wind, touching the leaves in the maples and rustling the grass as though some creature that belonged only to the night had passed on its way to some mysterious and secret place. There were the dew-wet scents of roses and newly cut grass, the night's own special blend, a rare and precious perfume.

It was the kind of night that sends even cats who have known many midsummer nights cavorting among the flowers like kittens. And as for kittens, they are completely filled with abandon, perhaps reaching far back over the centuries of their evolution to who knows what nocturnal fancies.

We were both young, my cat and I, filled with the simple joy of the night. For me there was also the unfounded feeling, so common to youth, that the future, perhaps even the world, was mine for the taking.

I was finished with school, and Nez and I were filled with the excitement of our first apartment back in Staunton where we had both graduated from high school, and where the family had lived for so long.

Nez had finished her post-high-school education and was working as a darkroom technician at the local hospital. She was a pioneer in the field, making the job easier for those blind women and men who would follow her over the years to come.

As for me, I'd finished my work at college, where I'd studied counseling, although I hadn't found a job, at least not one that paid. But I was working as a volunteer counselor and music therapist at a school for the retarded, and I played the piano at our little church. Even though the future held a measure of uncertainty, it stretched out before me as magical and beckoning as that mysterious, beautiful night.

An ambulance moaned along Augusta Street on its way to the hospital. The mournful wail brought me back, at least in part, from my world of dreams.

You came out to call Miss Muffet, I reminded myself, knowing deep inside that I probably wouldn't see her until the next day. She preferred the freedom of the outdoors to the snug security of the apartment, even on snowy nights, and this night would be irresistible.

Miss Muffet had been born free perhaps on just such a night, free to come and go at her pleasure, with the whole world her home. As far as I know her mother never had a name—well, not what anybody would call a proper name. Like Miss Muffet, she was a gray cat with white stripes. Probably she was one of those millions of cats, unloved and unwanted, who are left to their fate—along the highway, in housing developments, almost anywhere. Their owners are rid of the responsibility, and those who care enough to fool themselves into feeling good about it try to assure themselves that their abandoned pets have found a home.

Whatever her origins, she showed up at the kitchen entrance of Battle Hall. She had found a home—and what a home it was! Not for her the begging for scraps or the dodging of kicks and thrown objects that often befall strays. That cat had found a good thing, and she knew it.

Madalene, who was in charge of the food service, was a cat person from way back. She immediately took her in, both literally and figuratively. Every day that kitchen turned out meals for approximately two hundred people, and no matter how frugal she was, Madalene always had all kinds of wonderful odds and ends that had to be thrown out. The very best of these found their way to the cat's dish.

And as for love! I feel I'm safe in saying that no cat on this earth ever had more love than that one. Not only was there Madalene and her staff to pamper her, but there were somewhere in the neighborhood of one hundred and seventy students, little and big, all wanting a chance to pet her too.

This could be one reason the poor thing never had a name. Can you imagine the confusion of that many people trying to name a cat? We had suggestions ranging from Amethyst to Zenith. In the end, though, she and her offspring were always known simply as the Battle Hall Cats.

And of course there were offspring, who in turn produced their own offspring. Those cats would soon have outnumbered the students, except for the combined efforts of everybody concerned.

The chief recipient of kittens seemed to be Betty Fenwick, who taught music. Her studio was directly across the hall from my room in Battle Hall, and "I'm taking one of the kittens home" was heard with regularity as Betty went toward the stairs.

Miss Muffet was a Battle Hall Cat, and although she was only about six months old when Nez and I adopted her, she never got over those first months of complete freedom. On the worst of snowy days, she would run from one door to the other in the vain hope that the sun would be shining somewhere out there.

So that night I stood there in the warm, scented darkness, knowing that I probably wouldn't see her until morning, but knowing, too, that I would have to make the effort.

"Kitty, kitty, kitty. . . Miss Muffet," I called in my most persuasive tone. "Come on, pretty Muffet."

Finally I was rewarded by a far-off "*mew, mew!*"

It wasn't her usual somewhat disgusted call when she knew she'd had it and it would be a good idea to get herself home. It was a rather strange half call. As I continued to call, it grew closer and closer until, claws scrabbling on the rough wood of the steps, four little paws took their owner past me and into the kitchen at high speed.

I backed through the open door and slammed it, remembering countless nights when she had changed her mind just as I'd followed her inside.

"You're such a good girl," I crooned. "You came straight home, and—"

I froze as my hand closed not on the short-haired half-grown cat I had expected, but on a somewhat matronly long-haired creature. She immediately began to purr, her head turned toward the dish of Friskies.

"Did she come?" Nez called from the bedroom where she was laying out her clothes for work the next day.

"Sort of," I said, just as Mrs. Cat—well, I had to call her something—abandoned the Friskies and started toward Nez's voice at a pace that wouldn't have shamed a cross-country runner.

"What do you mean?" Nez asked, her voice now coming from the hall.

"Uh, she came. Only, she isn't Miss Muffet."

Now, Nez likes cats, but gentle, friendly cats are definitely her style. There was no way of knowing whether Mrs. Cat fit into that category. That she was friendly was pretty evident from the way she came sprinting through the back door. And if you could believe the way she purred, even when pounced on by a stranger, she was gentle. But with cats, it's not always easy to go by appearances. I once knew a cat named Skeater who would gently lick the spot she was getting ready to nip.

"But who is she?" There was both concern and curiosity in the question. Nez reached out a timid hand to stroke the dangerous creature purring around her feet.

"You've got me," I said, yawning. "She came along behind the houses. Unless somebody in the neighborhood just got a new cat, she doesn't belong to one of the neighbors. Also, I think that if somebody just got her, they'd keep her in. Somehow, I have the feeling she's lost."

By then the cat had given up her purring and had settled herself on Nez's bed, from which she was determined not to move.

"Oh, well," Nez said, carefully settling beside her, "whoever she belongs to will probably come looking for her in the morning."

But morning brought no calls of "kitty, kitty" as her owner came searching for her, and inquiries through the neighborhood netted no information except that nobody had ever seen her before.

Of course, somebody could have brought her to the area and abandoned her, especially since she was very definitely expecting kittens. Somehow, and even now I don't know why, I didn't think so. She was friendly and gentle enough even for Nez, and she had been trained to a litter pan. Although her long (silver gray, a neighbor told me) coat was snarled from her journey, she was accustomed to being groomed. That was obvious from the way she happily jumped on my lap when she saw the grooming brush. Wherever her other life had been, love and care had been an important part of it.

"We can't keep her," I told Nez when she came home that afternoon. "She won't even let poor Muffet come up the back steps. She's an affectionate cat, and she isn't about to share us with anybody else."

"But this is Muffet's home," Nez protested, echoing my own feelings.

"I know that, you know that, Muffet knows that—but try and convince Mrs. Cat. No, even if we had room in this small place for another cat, it just wouldn't work. We either have to find her owner or find a good home for her."

But who will want a cat about to have kittens?

I didn't ask that one out loud. Nez is one of the most tenderhearted creatures on this or any other planet, and that was one complication I didn't need. I was feeling bad enough myself.

The next morning I set about finding out what to do with a homeless cat. My first discovery was that at that time we didn't have an SPCA to cushion the process.

"Take the broom to her," one elderly vet, accustomed to large-animal practice, advised. "She'll go somewhere else. Don't feed her!"

Behind me I heard the contented sound of Mrs. Cat crunching away at the food dish in the kitchen. I hung up in a hurry.

"Call the police," the assistant in my own vet's office advised when I finally got through to her around nine-thirty. "They'll take her to the city pound. They'll take care of her there until you can find her owners or, failing that, a good home for her. If nobody claims her, let us know and we'll help you find a home. She sounds like at least part Persian."

So, feeling worse than Benedict Arnold must ever have felt, I called the police department. The officer who answered assured me that somebody would be right over.

"Now, don't you take any chances, lady," he advised me. "You never know what a strange cat might do. I'll get a man right over with a net."

"She isn't—"

But he'd already hung up.

"I have a feeling this isn't going to work," I told the sunny July morning as I went to give Mrs. Cat a final brushing.

If the Staunton police department was as prompt at answering all its calls as it was answering that one, the crime rate should have been low, to say the least. I carried Mrs. Cat on my shoulder to answer the front doorbell, promising her and myself that, somehow, I would find a home for her.

"I came to pick up a stray cat," a deep voice informed me.

"Well—well, I— Well, I may have changed my mind," I

stammered, holding her closer. Before I could say anything else, I heard the officer catch his breath.

"Why, that's my cat! Pie?"

I felt her move her head at his voice, and then she was in his arms. I'm sure you could have heard her purring at the other end of the apartment.

"It *is* Pie!" he cried, joy in every syllable. "She disappeared the day before yesterday, and we've been looking everywhere for her. Where did you find her?"

"I didn't. She found us, my sister and me. We're both blind, and before we knew what was going on, she had come running in and taken over the house. And our hearts, too, I'm afraid. We have a cat, though. Besides, we felt that she had to be somebody's pet. We were going to put an ad in this afternoon's paper."

"I just can't believe it," he said. "I live miles from here, way out in the country. I probably wouldn't even have thought about answering your ad."

"How do you suppose she got here?" I asked. I could hardly believe it, either.

"The only thing I can think of is that she must have been on the top of my car when I left for work that afternoon, and I didn't notice her. She probably jumped off somewhere around here when I stopped for a light."

"She must have recognized a sympathetic soul when she heard me calling our cat." I smiled, feeling that I was a part of one of life's little miracles, the kind that are so often written off as coincidence.

"I don't know how to thank you for taking such good care of her." I could hear him take out what was probably a wallet.

"Thank us by doing the same for somebody else," I said. "Our cat means a lot to us. I'd like to think that if she were lost, somebody would look after her."

"The kids have been praying every night that she'd come

home, but my wife and I were afraid we'd never see her again. We didn't tell them that, of course."

"And God heard," I said, giving Mrs. Cat—Pie—a last pat as they went through the door.

I was remembering another time, another place, and another cat. "God always hears." Mama's words seemed to come to me down the years.

I had learned so many lessons since that long-ago day, and I smiled as I thought about the joyous lesson of a prayer answered that those unknown children were about to learn.

A loud bang came from the back door, followed by Miss Muffet's demanding "*meow, meow!*"

"I'm coming, I'm coming," I called. There had been no reason to ask God to bring Miss Muffet home, and I made a mental note to call Nez at work as soon as I had fed her.

Things were back to normal—at least, as normal as they ever were in our household—and I gave the protesting Miss Muffet a hug.

11

"Such a Good Little Cat…"

Hope against hope and ask till ye receive.

JAMES MONTGOMERY

I have heard it said that moving ranks as high as divorce when it comes to trauma, and some fainthearted souls have added death to the list. Whether you go that far or not, it can't be denied that to pack everything and transport it somewhere else is something of an experience all by itself, not to mention looking for all those things you know you put in just the right box so they would be easy to find. But if you're blind and live with a blind sister, and if you have an eccentric cat— Well, it might be a good idea to go ahead at the beginning and call the proverbial little man in the white coat or, better still, stay where you are.

Nevertheless, just to prove that I probably need not just

one of those little men but a whole army of them, I like to move. Oh, I could do without all the packing and unpacking and searching, but there is something exciting about living in a different place. There is the thrill of exploring to see just where to put everything and the joy of finding a spot where you can put something new. This last is always a priority for the blind with our mountains of Braille books.

There are new neighbors, both human and animal, and there is the atmosphere, the very feel of the place.

Who has lived and loved and laughed under that roof? What words of love or hate have those ceilings echoed back? What dark secrets of the past lie there, forever hidden from the outside world?

So it was with mixed emotions that I began to pack that summer of 1964.

"But I thought you liked it here," Lib Houser said. She lived two houses up, and was stunned when I told her we were looking for another apartment.

"We do like it." I rescued my coffee from Miss Muffet's prying nose, and managed to drop the phone in the process. Muffet gave up on the coffee, and I heard her jump to the top of the television.

"Phyllis?" Lib's voice came from under the bed.

"Sorry," I said, retrieving the telephone. "Where were we?"

It says much for our relationship with the Housers that Lib didn't bother to ask what had happened. No doubt she had heard Muffet's insistent meow, and thought it was better not to ask.

"You were telling me that you're going to move, and I was asking why."

"Nez has lost her ride to work," I explained. "We've tried to work it out, but there just isn't any other way. It sounds silly to move when we live just a few blocks away, I know."

"It doesn't sound silly to me. I don't like to walk along this street, and I can see. Everybody keeps hoping they'll put in sidewalks, but I don't think they ever will."

Although Ray's eye condition has improved so that he can drive a car, he was one of the "big boys" when I first went to school, and it seems that we've known each other all our lives. Lib and Ray, along with their two children, Linda and Donnie, were perfect neighbors—there when you needed them and absent when you didn't.

At that time, Ray worked at WTON, one of our local radio stations, on Saturday afternoons. His "Ray's Romper Room" was something of an event for all of us, including the cats, our Miss Muffet, and the Housers' Rover. Yes, I said cat, and nothing else needs to be said for the wry sense of humor of a man who would name his cat Rover. Miss Muffet would sit beside the radio and meow loud enough to be heard downtown at the station whenever Ray said something about her on the air. It seemed to us that she knew when he would be broadcasting, even those programs such as his "Sacred Songs" where she wasn't mentioned.

The Housers, all four of them, had seen us through countless emergencies, and now was no exception. They didn't want us to move, Lib said, but she would help us look for a place.

And right on cue I heard their back door bang as Ray, also the moving force in Ray's Vending, came charging in. He had just finished servicing the machines that dispensed sandwiches, coffee, you name it.

"Is that Pete?"

No, I don't know, and neither does he, why he ever started calling me Pete, or Petie, but he did, and still does.

"Yes, but, Ray—" Lib's voice was cut off as he took the phone from her.

"What were you and Nez doing, walking along the side of Augusta Street?" he demanded. "I was caught in traffic so I couldn't stop, and I was afraid to yell at you. You were in enough danger without a distraction."

His usually good-old-boy voice was stern. "Don't you know that's a good way to get killed? I mean, if you don't step in a hole, or get bitten by somebody's dog, you're sure to get hit by a Mack truck."

"Nez has lost her ride to work," I said meekly. "We were walking the route, hoping it wasn't as bad as we'd thought."

"Well, ain't that a crock," he said, good humor partly restored, along with his intentionally bad grammar. "I thought you'd lost your marbles, or something. But she doesn't plan to walk to work!"

"No," I said with a deep sigh. "Ray, we'll have to find somewhere else to live, and the irony of it is that it could be way on the other side of town."

"Yeah, I know. But if the city bus runs somewhere close, she can ride right to the door of the hospital. It's awful to be blind, ain't it, Petie?" He ended with the humorous line that always won us a laugh. I'm not sure who said it first, but somehow it lightens up almost any situation that just might make us feel sorry for ourselves.

"We'll help you find a place," he promised, and I could hear the rustle of the newspaper as Lib started to look.

In the end, though, it was Winnie Ayres who helped us find that four-room apartment with high ceilings and bay windows. We had known Winnie and her husband, Raymond—Grandma and Uncle Raymond, as we called them—for some time, but it was through Raymond's nephew, Ed Thurston, that the acquaintance blossomed into a friendship that in many ways was stronger than family ties.

To quote Ed, he wandered into our lives one Saturday in early spring 1963, "and things have never been quite the same." Ed had come to town to take the position of home teacher for the Virginia Commission for the Blind, and although a home teacher is now called a rehab teacher, and the commission has become the Virginia Department for the Visually Handicapped, Ed remains the same—fun loving, considerate of the needs of others, always there. In short, another brother.

We always said that Ed could see just enough to get him into trouble, and he proved it on that first day by sitting in the chair I offered—right on Muffet.

Grandma and Uncle Raymond would not have appeared on the social register or in *Who's Who,* but they occupied a prominent place in many hearts. They didn't own a car, but they visited the sick and those in need more than anybody I've ever known. They walked when they could and took a cab when they couldn't. It would be impossible to say just how much of their small income they spent in "doing" for others, because it was equally impossible to know just how much they did, and they never told anybody.

It was natural, then, that when they heard we were looking for an apartment, Grandma joined in the search.

"Come have dinner with us Sunday after church," she said on Saturday evening. "I can read the apartments-for-rent ads to you. There are a lot of them in the Sunday paper. If any are close, Raymond and I can walk over there with you. Edward's visiting his parents this weekend, so there'll be just us."

By that time, Ed was living in the other half of the house they rented, and we usually ate together when we visited on Sunday.

After we'd finished eating, and eating, and eating some more, Grandma began to look through the newspaper.

"Here's one," she said with enthusiasm. "It's on East Frederick Street, right down the street from the Woodrow Wilson birthplace."

"That could be one of Mr. Cro's houses," Nez said.

Like Miss Lena Delinger, Mr. Cronise had come to the

school as a pupil and stayed on to teach. Unlike Miss Lena, he had been married, and he owned not only the house where he lived but also two others, which he rented.

When his wife died just before his retirement, we were all afraid that he would soon follow her. They had been inseparable, and I'm sure no one could imagine how lonely he must have been. But he was made of sterner stuff, and to our amazement he remarried, a somewhat younger woman who had been a friend of theirs for many years.

"I'll look in the phone book," Grandma said. "I think it's the house next door to his. If it is, I know he owns it."

And it was the house next door. Fearing that the apartment had been rented, I dialed the number Grandma read to me.

"Well, Miss Staton—and Miss Staton," came Mr. Cronise's familiar voice. "Miss Inez and Miss Phyllis. I haven't seen you girls in a long time."

I told him that we had heard about his ad and were interested in the apartment.

"I don't do business on Sunday," he said, "but you come on over and Mrs. Cronise will show it to you. Afterward, we'll talk and maybe have some music. Have you got time to play a little for us?"

"Of course."

I'd have played all night if it meant getting an apartment that close to the bus line, and close to downtown besides.

"Do you like it, girls?" Mr. Cronise asked us half an hour later as we settled in rocking chairs around the center table in his living room while Mrs. Cronise served lemonade.

"We love it," we said together.

"Then, if you think the rent's fair, it's yours. I'm a little worried about that old stove, though. I think we'll buy you one like ours. Before you go home, Baby will take you back to the kitchen and show you ours."

I'd been worried about that museum piece, too, but had decided I would manage. Now there was another worry. I knew I'd have to face it. So, after a silent prayer, I plunged in.

"There's just one thing, Mr. Cronise." I took a deep breath. "We have a cat."

There, I'd done it. My announcement was met with dead silence.

"Well, now," he said finally in his slow, rumbling voice. "You know I don't allow pets. Wait—it isn't because I don't like them. It's because we're right on the street. The little daughter of one of my tenants was killed right there across the street, and I've never rented to people with children or pets since. They both need room to play in a place where they're safe."

"But she's really such a good little cat," I said. "She stays at home."

Forgive me, Lord, for that little lie, but You know how much we need this apartment, and how much that silly little cat means to us.

"Well. . . " he rumbled.

"I think it would be all right, Jimmy."

Mrs. Cronise had a soft, gentle voice that always seemed to get through to Mr. Cro, and now was no exception.

"Well, Baby, I don't know. But if you think it's all right."

"Cats aren't like dogs," she reminded him. "They don't bother anybody, and they stay at home."

Oh, yeah? I thought, remembering the countless times Miss Muffet had jumped fearlessly from a branch to the Housers' roof, only to realize she didn't have the nerve to jump back again.

"Oh, she's no trouble at all," Nez fibbed in her turn. "She's an affectionate little cat."

At least that part was the truth. Miss Muffet seemed to love everybody, and she lived content in the belief that everybody loved her in turn.

"She's one of the Battle Hall Cats," I added, as though that had anything to do with it.

"Then she ought to be used to blind folks," he said. "And she'll have Baby to keep an eye on her over here. She likes cats."

Sometimes, now, when I wake in the night and, as the song says, "count my blessings instead of sheep," I wonder what my world would be like if we hadn't decided to take that apartment.

12

Miss Muffet Pays Her Respects

*Good company and good discourse are the very
sinews of virtue.*

IZAAK WALTON

The September breeze lightly moved the bedroom curtains
with a soft rustle. It was early morning and the air was cool,
speaking of fall.

The cries of what sounded like hundreds of birds on their
way to their winter feeding ground filled the crisp air. Miss
Muffet jumped to the windowsill and trilled softly.

"You don't need to hunt your breakfast," I told her as I
picked her up and started toward the kitchen. Because she
had been a completely free spirit for almost the first year of
her life, she persisted in hunting, and no amount of good

food and scolding ever changed her. I don't think she ate any of her kills, but she stalked everything from snakes to pigeons and often proudly presented her trophies to me.

Not only did she delight in hunting, but nothing—and I do mean nothing—was as great to her as the chance to climb. She climbed everything, from trees to doors, to rooftops. She would climb *anything*.

"She's been everywhere in the apartment except the top of the deep freeze," I told Grandma Ayres one afternoon when we were shopping.

"Phyllis," Grandma said as we walked through the front door, "you won't believe it, but your cat is sitting on top of the freezer."

The trouble was, that although Miss Muffet was the world's champion climber, she seemed to know absolutely nothing about how to get down.

Nez and I had moved to our new apartment in July, repeating our assurances to Mr. Cronise that Miss Muffet was a good cat. Well, she was—but who's to say what that is? She didn't walk around on the dining room table or use the living room carpet for a litter box, and to me she was certainly a good cat. But I have a friend whose cat casually walks across the table after it has been set with the best linen and china, and she, too, is a good cat. In short, if you love cats, you will usually forgive them anything.

The problem was that we couldn't be sure just how Mr. Cronise felt about cats.

"But he always had dogs," Nez reminded me right after we moved. "Remember Blackie?"

Blackie had been almost as much of a fixture as Robin at the Virginia School for the Blind. Every morning he would walk with Mr. Cronise to school, then patiently wait outside his classroom until he was ready to go home in the afternoon. One afternoon, though, Mr. Cronise rode home with one of the other teachers instead of walking the four blocks.

He went straight on to tune a piano at one of the local churches, and when he got home around six o'clock, he was distressed to find that Blackie wasn't there. He had just started to call the school switchboard when his telephone rang.

"Mr. Cronise, this is Mabel Chandler, the maid at the girls' dormitory. Have you missed Blackie?"

"Yes, Miss Mabel, I have. Is he over there?"

"Yes, sir. He's outside your classroom and he won't leave. I'd be glad to bring him home, but he won't come with me."

"And I had to walk over there and get him," Mr. Cronise would always say when he told the story. "He was so glad to see me. He had been waiting all that time for me to come back. I suppose when he saw me get in Mrs. Davis's car, he didn't realize I was going home."

"Surely he likes and understands cats," Nez said as we remembered Blackie.

I wasn't so sure, though. After all, there are those who love cats and those who love dogs, and like East and West, never the twain shall meet.

But as time passed and Miss Muffet remained a good cat, even winning words of praise from Mr. Cronise, we began to relax. Maybe the new apartment, with its high ceilings and large rooms, had made the difference. Cats do change, don't they?

So far as we knew she hadn't climbed a single tree, and there had been only one dead pigeon left next to the trash can. Yes, she was a changed cat.

How was I to know on that September morning as I opened a can of Nine Lives that the period of peace and change had ended?

"Where's the cat?" Nez asked that night as she came out of the bathroom.

There was never the slightest doubt that Miss Muffet knew

we were blind. In fact, for a long time I think she was convinced that the entire human population was blind. I will never forget her consternation the night Lib caught her in the act of knocking the flower arrangement off the coffee table. Lib gave her a sound whack with a rolled newspaper. That had been one of Miss Muffet's favorite tricks from day one. She would knock the arrangement to the floor, then run like all the powers of darkness were chasing her, as indeed they were, in a way. But we never managed to catch her.

After that, she learned in a hurry who could see and who couldn't. One of her favorite games was to leap on some unwary blind person, preferably one with bare feet.

"I don't know where she is." I said, handing Nez her slippers. It never hurt to take precautions. "Didn't you let her in?"

"No. I thought you did."

So it started—that calling and coaxing, and threats to "leave you out all night," all delivered in something of a stage whisper, so I wouldn't wake up the whole neighborhood.

"She just isn't coming," I said after about an hour, "and I don't care. She's stayed out all night before, and she can do it again."

They were brave words, but about every hour I'd slip out to the back porch, and then to the front porch, whispering, "Muffet. . . kitty, kitty. . . Muffet."

At six A.M. I was really worried when no soft form, damp from the dew, came running through the door. If it had been on Augusta Street, where she had countless cat friends and where the Housers often took her in, I wouldn't have worried, but she had never stayed out all night on Frederick Street. Mr. Cronise's warnings about the dangers of the street crowded in to take away my appetite.

"But she wouldn't go to the street." Nez tried to reassure me, and I heard her put down her piece of toast, probably untasted too.

"Of course she wouldn't," I agreed. But we were both afraid she had.

Just then the phone rang. Praying for good news, I went to answer it. In my heart, though, was the fear that Miss Muffet was out there in the street, dead or dying, and somebody had called to tell us. *Please, God,* I prayed silently, *don't let that be it. . . .*

"Miss Phyllis." It was Mr. Cronise's voice, sounding deeper than ever, hoarse with sleep. "You owe me for a night's lodging."

"Sir?"

Had he taken leave of his senses? Had senility set in overnight? Not Mr. Cronise!

"All right," I said, trying to make my voice soothing. "How much is it?"

Good heavens! Would I have to pay him? And what on earth had put such an idea into his mind?

Then I heard his familiar chuckle. "Actually, you don't owe me a thing. But that cat owes me ten dollars for a night's lodging, because she spent the night in my house."

Relief surge through me. He was all right. No awful thing had happened to his sanity. And then what he had said got through, and some of my euphoria slid away.

"What do you mean?" I asked, but I didn't think I really wanted to know.

"She spent the night over here. Baby woke me up around three o'clock and told me she heard her, but I told her to go back to sleep."

"I knew I heard her." Mrs. Cronise's voice came over the extension.

"You heard her?"

"Yes," she said. "I heard her bell."

Miss Muffet's bell had been one of our attempts to keep track of her whereabouts. Unfortunately, she had learned—

and learned in a hurry—how to hold her head perfectly still when she didn't want it to ring.

"But where was she?"

"Jimmy said she was on the porch, and finally we went back to sleep," Mrs. Cronise said.

"She woke me up again about dawn." Mr. Cronise picked up the story. "And there she was in our bedroom, standing by the bed and looking at Baby."

"Good heavens!"

I still shiver to think what could have happened if Miss Muffet had jumped on the bed while they were still asleep. Can you imagine waking up to find a furry thing with claws on your bed? People have had heart attacks from less.

"How did she get in?" I asked.

"Probably through an upstairs window," Mrs. Cronise said. "When Betty Sue, who rents our upstairs apartment, came home last night, she found her in the hall. She thought we were cat sitting, so she didn't put her out. Betty Sue says her kitchen window was open."

I sighed. Miss Muffet was up to her old tricks again. "I'm sorry," I apologized, remembering how good I had said she was.

"That's all right," Mr. Cronise said. "We'll have to give her a chance to get used to her new home. You just tell her she owes me for a night's lodging. I have a feeling she doesn't pay her debts, so we'll write it off."

They hung up, laughing. I, like Queen Victoria of England, wasn't amused. Miss Muffet wasn't getting used to her new home. That was what she had been doing while she was on her best behavior for the past month. Now that she was used to her new home, she was her old adventurous self!

As I replaced the receiver, I wondered what would come next. I didn't have long to wait.

"Miss Phyllis." This time Mr. Cronise didn't sound so benevolent.

"Good morning." I tried to make my voice brisk and cheerful. Maybe he was only calling to tell me that our favorite Braille magazine had come.

"That cat's over here again. She was on the porch when I went to get the mail, and when I came back in the house she ran in. She didn't make a sound until she got inside. Then she shook her bell, tipped me with her tail, and ran like a thief."

Apparently Miss Muffet had discovered that he was blind too.

"I'll be right there."

I didn't tell him that there was no way I could catch her if she wanted to spend the day on a social call. Happily, I didn't have any trouble. Well, not much. She let me chase her around the house twice. Then she walked over to rub around my legs.

For Miss Muffet, this was the best game yet as she managed to stay just out of reach while she watched two blind humans wandering around searching for her or madly chasing her. It had to be great fun, because she repeated the game just about every week. Soon I began dreading the sound of my landlord's voice on the phone.

After a while, though, I think we both began to look forward to those days when Miss Muffet gave us the perfect excuse to drop whatever we were doing and sit and talk. Or, in my case, listen as Mr. Cronise took me back in time to a place where things moved more slowly and when there had been the time to sit as we were sitting, rocking and remembering, talking about many things or maybe just enjoying a comfortable silence. Today I bless that meddlesome, naughty little cat who, in her own way, knew how to enjoy life to its fullest.

I was afraid that it was about to end, though—all the closeness, all the talk, all the goodwill—on a rainy night in November.

The house where Nez and I lived had, many years before, belonged to our old friend Dr. Bradford, the school doctor. He had lived in the main part of the house and maintained his office where we now had our apartment. The rest of the house, about six rooms on two floors, was rented out as an efficiency apartment and single rooms. To say that Mr. and Mrs. Cronise were selective about who rented from them would be to put it mildly. So when they told me that evening that they had rented to a new man, I didn't think much about it. We had two private entrances, so we seldom saw the other tenants.

It must have been around midnight that we heard the shriek coming from upstairs.

"What on earth was that?" Nez asked as we both jumped out of bed.

Then everything was as quiet as the tomb except for the tap of sleet at the windows.

"Should we call the Cronises?" Nez asked.

"No," I said around a yawn. I had a feeling, a strong feeling born of experience, that "that cat" had something to do with it.

I was right. The next morning Mr. Cronise was on the phone as soon as his wife left for work at one of the county schools where she taught the first grade.

"Miss Phyllis, I'd like to see you."

I couldn't tell just what his mood was, but I walked as slowly as possible to his house next door.

"Do you know the new man?" he asked without any preliminaries.

"I haven't met him, sir," I said in my most respectful voice.

"He came over this morning before Baby went to work, and he told me that cat was in his bed last night."

That tears it! I thought. *We and "that cat" are on our way out.*

"I'm sorry." I meant it from the bottom of my heart. "I called her, and when she didn't come, I finally went to bed. Was the man very upset?"

What a stupid question!

"You might say that."

And, to my amazement, Mr. Cronise began to laugh. Not his usual chuckle, but a loud, deep-down laugh.

"He must have left his door open while he went to the bathroom. When he came back, he got under the covers—and there was something warm and fuzzy."

I tried to laugh, too, but I was still worried. "I'm so sorry," I apologized. "I know Muffet has been a lot of trouble, and I know I told you what a good cat she is, and—"

He took my hand in his big warm one, made strong yet gentle by years of coaxing beauty and harmony from neglected pianos. "Now, now, Miss Phyllis, it's all right. She's your pet, and I know she means a lot to you both. To tell the truth, I owe her something, because that man drinks. I smelled it on his breath this morning, and if he starts drinking that early, he has a problem. We might not have suspected until there was trouble. Now we'll be on the alert. You know I don't allow things like that in my house."

Relieved, I sat down in the old rocker. Following an instinct, I reached down to find Miss Muffet just about to jump on the piano. As I lifted her to my lap and started to rock, Mr. Cronise began what I loved the most, his stories of the school and the town as he remembered them. As he talked and took me back to times gone by—to a past that now existed only in the minds and hearts of those who had lived it—I said a prayer of thanks for people like him and Miss Lena, who had lit the path for all of us who came after them. And for the first time, I found myself wondering about those who might follow me.

13

Enchantment on a Rainy Night

The human heart, at whatever age, opens only to the heart that opens in return.

MARIA EDGEWORTH

It was Saturday, December 19, 1964, the coldest day of the year. Maybe the coldest day in the history of the planet if the temperature of my hands could be believed. I found myself wondering if the tears on my cheeks might soon freeze.

I don't usually cry at weddings. I've played for too many of them over the years. But this one was different. It was Nez moving sedately down the aisle on Ray Houser's arm in time to the bridal music from Wagner's *Lohengrin*. It was Fay sitting there where Mama would have sat. It was Billy Wine waiting for Nez at the altar.

While my hands moved instinctively over the familiar chords, my tears fell unchecked. They were tears of joy and sorrow, all mixed up in one soggy bundle.

Nez and I had known and liked Billy for more years than we could count, but it had been only the summer before that he and Nez had discovered their love. It is a love that has endured in spite of job changes, illness and near-death, and the fact that they are both blind.

"I think it's wrong to have a house without windows," some would-be humorist once said of a marriage between two blind people. He was wrong. Love—the kind of love Nez and Billy share—can bring warmth and light to the coldest and the darkest of places.

So my tears of joy were for them and the life they would share, while my tears of sorrow were for myself. We had always been together, Nez and I, and although Billy was as dear as any brother, I knew that things would never be quite the same. I knew, too, that change, that joyous kind of change, is what makes the world the wondrous place it is.

Nez and Billy would be moving away from Staunton, and I would go on living in the apartment Nez and I had shared. Of course we would talk on the phone and get together now and then. But visiting out of town isn't the same for those of us who are blind. A few miles can be a great distance. After all, we can't get in our car and drive off for a weekend, and even back then bus service between cities was becoming more difficult because the carriers were downsizing.

Nez and I had shared the expenses of the apartment with her salary and my allowance from what was then called Aid to the Blind. My allowance would be increased after her marriage, and I knew that if I was very careful, I'd be all right financially. But even if I were a millionaire, it wouldn't have made a difference. I was happy for my sister and her husband, but at the same time I felt sad.

I still had my job as pianist at the little church, and my volunteer work at the School for Retarded Children. My life had a purpose. Still, it wouldn't be the same without that sister who was a part of me, almost as though we were twins.

So the music soared, and my tears fell, and my life moved into yet another phase.

I was back in Montague Hall. Mr. Ham, the night watchman, hadn't come to turn on the heat, and I was freezing. The electric bell at the end of the big girls' hall was ringing insistently, and with a sick certainty, I knew I would be late for school.

Then Montague turned into the apartment Nez and I had shared. The cold winter morning turned into the early-morning chill of spring. And the bell became the telephone.

Grumbling about Mr. Cronise's frugal nature, which had made him turn off the heat in early April, I reached to lift the receiver.

"Miss Phyllis."

Maybe he had called to ask if I was cold. Not very likely. I'd known him and Baby to sit on the study sofa covered with a blanket on chilly spring or fall evenings rather than to reverse his decision about the furnace.

"Good morning," I said, trying to balance the telephone on my shoulder so that I could feel the hands of my Braille watch. Eight thirty! I'd overslept again.

"Baby was wondering if you'd like to come over for supper tonight," Mr. Cronise was saying. "We're having vegetable soup."

I was so glad that he hadn't called about another of Miss Muffet's escapades that I'd have agreed to anything, but this was something special. Homemade vegetable soup is one of my favorites, and nobody, except maybe Mama, could make soup like Baby's.

"I'd love to," I said, "but are you sure she feels like company? Is her cold better?"

"You aren't company. You're family. She said to tell you that you can bring the dessert." That is the kind of people they were. Mrs. Cronise knew that I had baked a pound cake the day before, and, aware that I'd probably feel another person would be a bother, she had given me an active part in the preparations.

"You've got a bargain," I told him, trying to make the telephone cord stretch into the dining room so I could turn on the percolator. I was running late again.

Billy and Nez had been married over a year. It was now, incredibly, May 15, 1966, although it seemed only a few weeks since that cold December day when they had exchanged their vows.

At the beginning of the spring semester, in February of 1966, I had started taking a business course at Dunsmore Business College. I hadn't been able to find a job, and my rehab counselor from the Commission for the Blind and I both hoped I would have better luck if I took this course.

Well, I thought as I poured dry food into Miss Muffet's dish while the coffee gurgled away, it was probably the closest I could come to my deep, almost-secret desire to become a writer.

"Forget about writing," my counselor had told me when I had timidly asked him about the availability of funds to study creative writing or journalism. "It isn't practical. You'll never make any money."

I supposed he was right, but in the quiet of the apartment at night when even the traffic along Frederick Street had dwindled to a few late cars, I wrote and dreamed in secret.

It had started as a way to fill my lonely evenings without Nez. Then, almost without my knowing it, the dream took root and grew quietly and steadily toward an eventual reality.

* * *

It rained all day. By the time I walked the short distance to the Cronises' house, the whole world seemed in imminent danger of floating away. It didn't dampen our spirits, though, and we had a lovely evening.

Around eight o'clock the rain slackened, and I decided that I should be getting home before it started again.

"I'll get my coat," Mrs. Cronise offered just as she sneezed twice.

"Please don't," I said. "There isn't a thing out there to hurt me, and you could get pneumonia. I'll be fine."

Just then the front door opened, letting in a blast of cold, wet air.

"Have you met our new roomer?" Mrs. Cronise asked.

Oh, no! Not another one, I thought, remembering the one who had found Muffet in his bed two years before. I was beginning to get paranoid. What would that cat do to this one? His living upstairs in the Cronises' house instead of the one where Miss Muffet and I lived wouldn't stop her. Muffet was no respecter of either people or houses.

"No, I haven't," I said aloud.

"Chuck Campbell, this is Phyllis Staton, who lives in our apartment next door," Mr. Cronise said.

"Hi, I'm glad to meet you." He took my hand in a firm grasp that, for some reason, made me feel excited and a little frightened. "I've seen you out with your cat."

Well, that was something. At least he hadn't said "that pest of a cat."

"Oh, everybody knows Miss Muffet." Mr. Cronise laughed. "She's quite a cat."

"She's a pretty cat," Chuck said. "I saw her in the Woodrow Wilson garden the other day. I think they were having a party, or something."

"A tea," I said weakly, remembering my encounter with the

woman who ran the gift shop at the Woodrow Wilson birth-place.

"I believe that striped cat is yours," she had said as she handed me the little sachet I'd bought for Grandma Ayres.

I didn't have to ask her to describe the cat further. I could tell from her disapproving tone that she wasn't pleased about something, and if a cat had displeased somebody, it was bound to be Miss Muffet.

My heart sinking, I wondered whether I should ask the woman why she wanted to know. She didn't bother to wait for the question.

"We were having a tea in the garden. The mayor's wife was there with guests from out of town. And *she* came. Your cat, I mean. There she was, walking around among the guests, begging anchovy paste—and people were giving it to her!"

I hadn't meant to say it. I really hadn't. It had just come out:

"How interesting. She never eats it at home."

We who live in Staunton are proud of the fact that President Woodrow Wilson was born here, and I suppose it didn't do a thing for the image of his birthplace to have a cat at the tea, but it had struck me as funny.

Now I stood there in the Cronises' study, shaking hands with this stranger with the firm touch and the interesting voice. I wondered what he would say if he knew how frivolous I was. And then I wondered what difference it made.

He was, after all, just one more person in the parade of tenants who rented a room for a time and then moved on. Probably, if he thought about me at all, he felt sorry for me, or thought how wonderful I was to manage so well. But I was willing to bet that he didn't see me as just another person—as a woman.

What on earth was wrong with me? For all I knew he might have a wife and a houseful of children tucked away somewhere. Or he could be a modern version of Jack the Ripper. I had let a strong, warm hand and a voice tinged with a smile do things to my imagination.

"I wonder if you'd do us a favor, Mr. Chuck?" Mr. Cronise asked. "Would you walk our Miss Phyllis home?"

"No, I'm fine. Really," I protested. Not too much, I hoped.

"Sure," Chuck said. "I'd be glad to whenever you're ready to go, but there's no hurry."

Fifteen minutes later, as we stepped onto the porch in front of my apartment, Chuck announced: "There's Miss Muffet sitting in your window."

"For once she's where she belongs." I unlocked the door. "Would you like to come in and be introduced formally?"

Without waiting for him to answer—he might say no—I moved aside and held the door.

"You're such a nice old cat," Chuck said, and I heard him lift Miss Muffet off her perch.

With those words, the attraction I'd felt from the second I had heard his voice became a strong, tangible thing. Somebody besides Nez and me, and of course Ray and Lib and their kids, truly admired that naughty little morsel of fur. I still don't know just how I knew, but I did know with certainty that Chuck, like us, would forgive her anything.

It is that simple sometimes—a word, a gesture, a feeling of kinship can touch and change our lives forever. And it was like that then, on that night of wind and rain, with the cars swishing along Frederick Street and Miss Muffet making noises like a mini buzzsaw.

"Do you have any pets?" I asked as we settled ourselves on the sofa with Muffet between us. Then I realized how silly that was. Of course he didn't, not in that one room at the back of the Cronises' second floor.

But to my surprise, he said, "Yes. I have a dog, Miss Bootie. She's at my stepmother's. She lives out next to the flower shop where I work. I lived there, too, until Dad—C.G., I always called him—died several years ago. He started the business, and I worked with him."

Then my mind made the connection. I remembered his father—at least, I remembered his flowers. The shop, River Hill Gardens, had done the flowers for the senior dance. In fact, River Hill did the flowers for every important occasion at the school. I remembered that Ray had told me that Mr. Campbell had died, and I had felt a stab of sadness at the loss of his kindness and creativity. Now, here I was, sitting next to his son on my own sofa.

"I'm leaving the business, though," Chuck was saying. "I'm studying drafting. It isn't the same without C.G." I heard the sadness, the loss, in his voice.

"I feel that I knew him in a special sort of way," I said. "He did so many lovely pieces for the school. One of the last things he did for me before I left was a wrist corsage. I played for the soloist at the senior dance."

Sitting there, I could almost smell those roses, feel their velvet softness, and hear the notes of "Over the Rainbow" as they flowed from beneath my fingers.

Chuck reached over and took my hand. "I did that," he said, speaking quietly. "I remember the tiny size. It was for your left wrist. They told me you were going to play the piano."

"Do you really want to leave the flower business?" I asked. He, too, would be a loss in a profession that was all too often losing the touch of individuality that had characterized his father's work.

"Yes." He sighed. "The shop has been sold, and I think it's time for me to move my life along. I wish I knew what to do about Bootie, though. My stepmother, Grace, doesn't like dogs, and Bootie knows it. She's always running away."

"Maybe you can find a good home for her," I suggested, feeling like a hypocrite. I wouldn't want to "find a good home" for Miss Muffet.

"Maybe. But we've been together a long time."

"Hey, I've got to get going," he added briskly a moment later, as though to push away the sadness I knew he must be feeling.

"Would you like to come for dinner tomorrow night?" I asked as I handed him his jacket.

I really hadn't meant to ask, although the thought had been lurking there ever since he had taken my hand in those gentle fingers. "Nothing fancy, but Muffet and I would love to have you."

"Thanks." The smile was back in his voice. "I don't get a home-cooked meal very often. Would you like to go out to see Bootie one day—and meet Grace, of course." He added the latter name without much enthusiasm.

"I'd love to. See you tomorrow."

And so it had started, the friendship, the sharing, and the understanding that would blossom like his beautiful flowers—and change our lives forever.

14

Bootie the Protector

The grandest of heroic deeds are those which are performed within four walls and in domestic privacy.

JOHN PAUL RICHTER

"She's done it again," Chuck said, and I heard him replace the receiver. He walked slowly back to the dining room and sat in a chair at the table.

I didn't have to ask who or what he was talking about. I'd been able to tell from Grace's tone when she asked to speak to him that she was displeased. It didn't take many smarts to know that the chief source of Grace's displeasure was usually either something Chuck hadn't done or something Bootie had done. Since Chuck was sitting in my dining room and enjoying the first turnips of the fall, it had to be Bootie.

I believe that Grace was one of those unfortunate souls

who doesn't like animals. She did have a cat, but what a cat!

"My cat never goes outside," she told me with apparent pride the first time Chuck took me to meet her. Although the cat had a whole beautiful world to wander in before it would encounter heavy traffic, I kept quiet. After all, it was her cat. Then her next words almost made me break my silence:

"I keep her in the bathroom."

"All the time?"

"Why, certainly," she said. "I have nice furniture. She comes out to eat."

I wondered then, and still wonder, what she wanted with a cat. But maybe she talked to the cat while she was sitting on the john or taking a bath. In any case, Bootie, a free spirit if I ever knew one, was miserable under such a rigid rule. She had been assigned the back porch for her quarters, and she ran away, probably looking for Chuck, at every opportunity.

"What does Grace want with a cat, or any other animal for that matter?" I had asked on the way home that first day.

"Who knows?" Chuck said. "She and C.G. were married only a few months when he died, and I've never understood her. To be honest, she probably doesn't understand me, either."

It is my belief that Grace, a retired registered nurse, resented anyone or anything she couldn't control. Both Chuck and Bootie fell into that category.

I thought about that as we sat in my dining room on that night in October, six months after we met. As the turnips turned cold on our plates, Chuck told me that Bootie had run away yet again.

"Grace says I'll have to do something about her," he went on, dejection in every syllable. "She suggested the SPCA, or that maybe I should have her put down. Phyl, I can't do that."

"You certainly can't!" I jumped up and started toward the closet to get my coat. "Supper can wait."

"Where are we going?" Chuck asked. A rustle of nylon told

me that he was taking his own jacket off the back of a chair.

"We're going to get Bootie, of course. She can live with Muffet and me."

I hadn't known I was going to say it—I really hadn't. But as the words came rushing out, I realized that the thought had been in the back of my mind for a long time.

"But what about Mr. Cronise?" Chuck asked.

There was that, of course, but the thought of strangers owning that loving little dog, or of the even worse alternative, pushed the consequences right out of my mind.

"I just won't ask," I said as we crossed the street to Chuck's car. "And if he tells me I'll have to move— Well, I'll find another apartment. Want to bet he won't say a word, though? He knows that if I have to move because of Bootie, you'll move too. Not to the same place, of course," I added quickly, feeling my face grow hot.

"It wouldn't be such a bad idea," he whispered as he slipped his arm around my shoulders. "Thank you. For taking Bootie, I mean."

And suddenly he was kissing me. It was a gentle, almost uncertain kiss, as though he thought it was wrong. Then, as I responded, he pulled me closer, and there in the cold October night, our spirits voiced the beginning of love.

It was a fragile thing, that unspoken emotion, made up of our loneliness and need, but it was there, a tiny flame warming our doubt, our mutual fear of a permanent commitment.

Chuck's parents had separated when he was seven, and he had fallen prey to all the uncertainty and feelings of guilt that burden the children of failed marriages. Could he risk a marriage of his own? As for me, there was always the fear that I couldn't take my place as a normal wife. Suppose I failed!

Later, on quiet evenings as we sat listening to the stereo, we shared our fears and doubts. We both knew that they were groundless. We knew it rationally, but, still, they were there in the secret places of our hearts, and only our love could banish them.

But on that October night, all that was in the future. *It was only one kiss,* I reminded myself as Chuck released me and we drove off to get Bootie.

So I got myself a dog, and if Mr. Cronise was displeased, he never mentioned it. I just acted as though his approval was an accepted fact, and after a week, I would have cheerfully moved rather than give her up.

They say that animals don't feel the same emotions as people do, and maybe they don't, but I know one thing: That dog was grateful. Maybe that sounds fanciful, but I know she was.

"You realize that she'll probably never do more than tolerate Muffet and me," I told Chuck on the way home that first night with Bootie sitting between us. "She's an older dog, and it's hard for them to get used to a new person. I'll take good care of her, though, and you can see her every day."

That just goes to show you how wrong I can be. From the first, Bootie was my little girl. If I went to the kitchen, she went to the kitchen. If I took a bath, there she was. When I played the piano or worked at my desk, she lay as close as possible to me. At night, though, she slept in the living room, seeming to know instinctively that the cozy spot on the foot of my bed belonged to Miss Muffet.

Like all my animals, Bootie didn't take long to find out that I couldn't see. But unlike Miss Muffet, she actually tried to protect me. She would push me with her nose if she saw me getting close to something, and she would do her best to scurry out of my way so that I wouldn't trip over her.

In January Mr. Cronise had a vacancy in the house where my apartment was, and he offered it to Chuck.

"It's a much nicer room," Mrs. Cronise told him. "And it will be closer to Bootie."

I've always thought that they realized the growing intensity of the feeling between us long before we did, but they never mentioned it.

My apartment had its private entrances in front and back, as well as a door opening into the hall in the main part of the house. Chuck was studying drafting through a correspondence course, and he found it convenient to come to my living room where he could study and pet Bootie all at the same time. At least, that's what we tried to tell ourselves.

Chuck usually parked his car at the back of the house, and we could go down the back steps and through the back gate to get to it. It was a route that was easy for Bootie and me to negotiate.

"Ready?" I called into the main hall one Saturday as we were preparing to visit Ed Thurston.

"Almost," Chuck called down the stairs.

"Okay. I'll take the extra set of keys and warm up the car."

Bootie scampered like a puppy down the back steps, across the yard, through the gate, and straight to the car.

"Here we go, girl," I said, opening the passenger's door for her. There was nothing she loved more than to go somewhere, anywhere, in the car.

I slammed the door and walked around to the driver's side. As I turned the key in the ignition, I heard a sad howl beside me.

"What on earth?" I asked, reaching out to touch Bootie. She was shaking like a leaf in a heavy wind, and trying her best to push me away from the steering wheel.

At first I wondered what had happened to her. Then I knew. Although I had started the car several times that winter while Chuck was getting ready, this was the first time she had been along. She knew I had no business driving a car. To her, if you sat behind the wheel, it followed that you were planning to move the car. She wasn't going to take any chances. Yes, indeed, Bootie had learned that I was blind. No doubt she, in her doggie way, thought she had saved both our lives.

But it was in the spring that Bootie became the heroine of the neighborhood.

Animals are like people. There are those, like Bootie, who find a place in your heart without trying, and there are others who turn you off from the beginning. The German shepherd who lived up the street fell into the latter category. All the women in the neighborhood were afraid of him, and I heard that he had killed a cat who belonged to someone on the next street. To make it worse, his master actually seemed to encourage his ferocity and made no effort to keep him at home.

One morning in early April, I heard a frantic pounding at my front door. Terror ran through me. I had let Bootie out a few minutes earlier, and although she never went to the street, she was the first thing I thought about as I rushed to the door.

"Phyllis, your dog!"

It was Shirley Venable, who lived in Mr. Cronise's basement apartment.

"What happened?" I asked, trying to keep my voice calm. Why hadn't I gone with Bootie!

"She chased that awful German shepherd."

It wasn't a car accident, thank heaven. Then I realized that it was excitement, even joy, in Shirley's voice.

"She chased him all the way home, nipping at his heels like he was a cow, or something! I always said that old dog was a coward. Here comes Bootie now."

"Bootie!" I cried as I heard her plop down in front of me on the porch. "Get in here before that dog realizes what was chasing him! He'd make two of you, girl."

"The little rascal," Chuck said that night when I told him about it. "C.G. taught her that when we had cattle. Has anybody said anything?"

I laughed. "Betty Sue from up the street stopped by and asked if she could buy Bootie a present. That German shepherd has terrorized the neighborhood for years, but so far, he hasn't left his front porch since his encounter with Bootie."

The dog did leave his porch after that, but he never again ventured to our end of the block. He had met somebody who wasn't afraid of him, and I'm sure he never forgot it.

So Bootie became a loved and valued part not only of my home but also of the neighborhood. Only one individual remained outside her circle of fans, and that was Miss Muffet. Oh, after the first couple of days, they maintained an uneasy truce, and Muffet formed the habit of sitting on Chuck's lap while Bootie lay on my feet, but it seemed that they each wished the other one were somewhere else.

Time moved on, through spring to summer to fall, and into winter. As the seasons passed, Chuck and I could no longer ignore our feelings. They were as much a part of us as the soft spring breeze or the wild wind of November.

"Are you sure?" I asked when, in August, Chuck asked me to marry him. He had finished his course a week earlier and had already found a job as an entry-level draftsman in nearby Charlottesville.

"Is anybody ever really sure?" he said, speaking into the silence that followed my question.

"Probably not," I admitted. "But you'll have to do things for me that you wouldn't have to do for a woman who can see."

"What things?"

And I realized with surprise that he meant it. Of course, he knew he would have to do all the driving, take me to the grocery store, and help me with countless other little things that most husbands take for granted. He knew because he had already done a lot of them, but it just didn't make a difference to him. And in that moment, listening to the question in his voice, I knew that it would work. It would work because we would make it work.

"I love you, Phyl," he said, the simple words brimming

with that love. "I love you, and I know you love me. You do, don't you?"

For the first time that hot summer evening, I heard doubt, even fear, in his voice.

"Oh, yes!" I said. "I love you, and I want to marry you more than anything on earth. I just want you to be happy."

And then we were holding each other, and there was only us, and the night filled with the music of crickets, and the scent of flowers coming from the backyard. Suddenly, something wet and insistent pushed between us. Tired of being ignored by the humans who were her life, Bootie had pushed her nose into the act.

"What about the wedding?" Chuck asked one evening in early September. "Do you want a church wedding?"

I almost giggled at the near-fear in his voice.

"Don't panic. You won't have to get all dressed up in a tux, or anything. A big wedding is an expense we don't need. You know my allowance will stop as soon as we're married, and, honestly, there's no such thing as a small church wedding. I mean, there's your mom and brother and sister in New Jersey—and can you imagine your mother and Grace sitting together in the same church? Seriously, we would have to invite all your family and all my family, not to mention all the people in the church where I play."

"But doesn't every woman want a big wedding?" he asked.

"Not this woman. I'd rather have a deep freeze or something else we'll be needing. Let's just have us, and Ed."

So we began to plan quietly. It was 1967, and we wanted to be married by the end of the year. After the wedding, Chuck would move into my apartment, and our new life would begin. Not very romantic, I suppose, but no bride and groom looking forward to a big wedding followed by a honeymoon in Europe could be happier than we were.

We planned the simple service for Friday night, December twenty-seventh. That way, we'd have the weekend together. Chuck hadn't been at his job long enough to take time off.

The days slipped by, and soon it was November. My mind was filled with happy thoughts about our plans that cold morning when I went to let Miss Muffet in. She had been up to her old tricks and had spent the night outside.

When I opened the back door, she came in slowly and went past her food dish, a thing almost unheard of. Something was wrong. I didn't know what, but when I touched her where she sat in her usual place on the living room radiator, I felt warm, sticky blood in her fur. My heart sank. What Mr. Cronise had always been afraid of had happened. Miss Muffet had been hit by a car or truck.

I carried her carefully to my bed, then called Dr. Simon, who had taken care of her since I got her.

"The doctor will be right there," Mrs. Simon told me. "Don't try to pick her up. A hurt animal can be dangerous."

I assured her that I wouldn't, not bothering to tell her that I already had.

"I'll come right now," Grandma Ayres said when I called her. "You need somebody who can see. If that doctor takes as long as people doctors do, it'll be a while."

But they both arrived about the same time.

"Will Bootie bite me?" Dr. Simon asked as I showed him into the bedroom.

"Where is she?" I'd forgotten all about her in the confusion.

"Sitting right beside Miss Muffet," he said, and I realized that she had been keeping watch over Miss Muffet while I'd been waiting for him and Grandma to come.

"Come, Bootie. Go with Grandma."

Grandma was one of Bootie's favorite people, but she wasn't about to leave Miss Muffet. Finally, I had to drag her away and shut her in the kitchen.

"Thank you," Dr. Simon said. "I didn't like the way she was looking at me." I heard him close the carrier.

"It's serious, isn't it?" I asked, trying to control my voice. I loved that meddlesome little cat.

"I'm afraid it is. But I could be wrong."

"Do whatever you'd do if she were your cat." It was hard to push the words out around the pain in my throat.

"I will," he promised. Neither of us said what that would be, although we both knew.

Dr. Simon called a little later to tell me that he had put Miss Muffet to sleep.

"I'm sorry," he added, "but her palate was crushed. There wasn't anything I could do."

I felt tears on my cheeks. "Mr. Cronise warned me about the danger of a car hitting her. But she survived a long time, and she brought a lot of pleasure. Thank you, Dr. Simon."

"Bootie will miss her too," he said. "They were such good friends."

As I hung up, I realized that he was right. I'll never know just when that friendship developed, but I have no doubt that it existed. Gentle, loving Bootie had been ready to fight for her friend as Miss Muffet lay dying on my bed. Only Bootie's discipline had kept her from defending Miss Muffet and keeping Dr. Simon at bay.

She was only a little brown dog with white boots. Her ancestry couldn't be traced, but if a blue ribbon were given for love and loyalty, Bootie would have won it paws down.

Just as I started to drift off to sleep that night, I felt the bed shake. Bootie had come for the first time and snuggled close to me. "Miss Muffet is gone," she seemed to say, "but you still have me."

"You're a wonderful girl," I whispered, burying my face in her soft fur. But she was already snoring.

15

Snowflakes
and Wedding Vows

*Of all earthly music, that which reaches farthest
into heaven is the beating of a truly loving heart.*

HENRY WARD BEECHER

It snowed the day before our wedding. The big, soft flakes blew against my face and stuck in my hair as Grandma and I turned the corner onto Frederick Street late that afternoon.

"Tomorrow's Friday, the twenty-seventh, isn't it?" she asked as I unlocked the door. We both paused to pet Bootie, who came bounding out of the dining room.

That Grandma! Chuck and I hadn't told her that we were going to be married the next day, but she knew. I don't know how, but she knew in that mysterious way she knew most things.

"Your hair looks pretty," she said, giving it a pat. "Miss Tucker did a real good job, but then she ought to. She's fixed your hair for two years now."

Miss Tucker had once owned her own beauty shop, but now she worked several days a week with Ann Fitzgerald, who had a shop in her home. Because of this, it didn't cost much, and even Grandma and I could afford to get our hair done.

Miss Tucker lived alone in a small apartment on Washington Street, where her only pleasures seemed to be her television set and her doll collection. She kept those dolls dressed more fashionably than she dressed herself. If she was surprised that I had kept my appointment in the midst of what amounted to a blizzard, she didn't say, but I think she knew too.

"There's no charge today," she had said when I opened my purse. "It's your Christmas present, and I want you to look nice."

We hadn't told anybody except Ed, and Roger Madden, the minister.

Roger and his wife, Noreen, and their two children had come to our little church in October.

"We can't tell anybody?" Noreen had asked.

"Not a soul," I insisted. "Noreen, will you stand up with us?"

"Of course, I will," she said, "but you know that everybody in the church would like to come."

"I know, I know," I said in mock despair. "Seriously, we want it this way. We don't want a big wedding, and I've seen too many little weddings turn into big weddings to know that this is the only way. Ed is going to be the only other person there."

"It will really be sort of fun." Noreen laughed. "I mean, I'll know something nobody else will."

So on that snowy Thursday, the last day I would spend as

Phyllis Staton, everything was ready. The simple service would take place at the church parsonage the next evening at seven o'clock. The gold wedding band was safely tucked away in my jewelry case, and my plain chiffon dress waited in my closet. If it would just stop snowing!

As I went almost fearfully to the kitchen the next morning, there was no need to wonder, because the first thing I felt was the reflection of the sun on my face. God had smiled on us, and as I started to make the coffee, I said a prayer of thanks, not only for the sunny day in spite of the snow, but also for that good man who would share my life, the man who so willingly offered not only himself but his eyes as well.

Tomorrow at this time we would belong to each other in the eyes of the world. We would call his family and mine, and our wonderful adventure would start.

"I now pronounce you man and wife."

Roger's usually fun-filled voice was solemn, and I heard a little sniffle coming from Noreen.

"No wedding was ever more pretty," she said when Chuck had kissed me gently and taken my hand. "I've seen more elaborate ones, but none where there was more love."

"We do have a lot of that," I agreed.

I'm afraid that I was already looking ahead with the rather unromantic thought that I'd have to remind Chuck that one of the local supermarkets had a sale on greens and spaghetti, ten cans for a dollar.

I have heard some couples claim that theirs is a perfect marriage. Well, perhaps it is. I suppose it depends on what you call perfect. If one means that those waters are never ruffled by difference of opinion or sadness, then ours isn't a perfect marriage. But if perfection is loving and respecting each other despite differences, and clinging even closer when the sad times come, then ours is decidedly perfect.

"But don't you feel guilty when you don't agree with him?" a blind friend asked me. "I mean, you have to depend on him to take you places, and read to you, and—well, so many things."

"Chuck doesn't feel guilty when he disagrees with me, even though he depends on me to fix his dinner and do the laundry," I said.

And that just about sums it up. We respect each other and we need each other. I do my thing and he does his.

The next few years slipped by, so quietly that sometimes I was surprised to see how much time had passed.

In March of 1968 I sold my first little piece to a magazine. It was a tiny check—fifteen dollars, I think—but no Pulitzer Prize winner was ever happier than I was. The short article, entitled "The Faith to Move Molehills," was sold to *The Warcry*, the publication of the Salvation Army.

"You sold something to a real magazine!" Chuck was more excited than I was when he came home that night and I told him.

"Here's the check!" I held out the envelope.

"Who read it to you? Do you know what the acceptance says?"

"I could tell it was one of my return envelopes, because I had put Braille on the inside," I explained. "And I could tell that they hadn't sent the manuscript back. I was just getting ready to get a cab over to Grandma's so she could read it, when I remembered that Carole Howell was next door."

Carole entered our lives when she married Elmer Howell, who had replaced Charlie and Shirley Venable as the tenants in the Cronises' basement apartment.

"I ran over calling Carole in so much excitement that Mr. Cronise probably thought the house was on fire. I think Mr. Cronise and Carole were as excited as I was."

"What are you going to do with your money?" Chuck pulled me down on his lap.

"Buy a new tablecloth," my practical self said without even stopping to think.

To my joy, this sale was followed by others, so that although I'd never be rich, I felt that my dream was coming true. Somebody liked what I had written, and liked it enough to pay me for it.

In 1969, our Bootie died suddenly of a stroke. I cried in secret for days, but the tears were for myself. Bootie had always been free in spirit, and now I felt that she was free of the arthritic body that had threatened to imprison her. She had been spared that, and I was grateful. But oh, how I missed her!

There was more sadness in store for us that year. It began on a hot summer evening with a phone call from Mrs. Cronise. "Something has happened to my Jimmy," she said, even in fear using her pet name for Mr. Cronise.

It was July third, and Chuck and I had been listening to a new recording of the Tia Juana Brass, reveling in the fact that we could sleep late the next day because it was a holiday.

"We'll be right there," I said, not bothering to put on a skirt over the shorts I was wearing because of the heat.

The rescue squad was on its way, and all I could do was hold Mr. Cronise's hand and try to comfort Baby. I knew with an instinctive, sinking certainty that he was dying.

Fifteen minutes later we were in the emergency room, and it was Baby's hand I was holding when the doctor came over with the terrible news. "I'm sorry," he said. "He had a massive heart attack. There was nothing we could do."

We took Baby home, and I started the sad chore of notifying friends and relatives. I would have to notify the rest of the tenants, too, and at Baby's direction assure them that "nothing would change."

That is the kind of woman she was, reaching out from her own grief to assure the tenants that, come the first of the month, they would still have a home.

In the days and months that followed, I did my best to console Baby, going with her to places where her Jimmy would normally have accompanied her, and doing my best to make her feel loved.

Late in 1970, she left the house where they had lived together and bought another house on North Augusta Street, several blocks north of where Nez and I had lived. We still saw her, of course, but things weren't the same. Still, I was glad to see that she seemed happier. She was building a new life, and our lives were moving on toward something I would never have dreamed of.

16

Crossing over Jordan

Our greatest glory is not in never falling, but in rising every time we fall.

CONFUCIUS

I sat on the dry summer grass, wondering for about the millionth time what I was doing there. The August sun made its way through the leaves like tiny jewels of heat and burned away the last of the night moisture.

Most of us think that the South—even states such as Virginia, which are not considered Deep South—is hotter than New York, but on that day, August 9, 1971, the temperature had topped ninety, and it was only a little after nine in the morning.

What was I doing here, surrounded by people and dogs? Why wasn't I back in our cool apartment, sitting at my desk, banging away on my faithful old Smith Corona, inventing situations, people, and animals for the stories I love to write?

Now you'll have a real-life story to write, I reminded myself silently.

Yeah, if I get out of this alive, the part of me that could be called either the voice of reason or the voice of pessimism chimed in.

And again I asked myself, *Why?*

"You need a dog," Bill Parker, a friend since grade school, had told me. That was on a day in early February. What amounted to a blizzard was blowing through Staunton. Bill and his dog guide, Elsa, were spending the weekend with Ed, and Chuck and I had made our sliding way across town to visit them.

"I don't think Mrs. Cronise would welcome any more pets," I told Bill. "After Bootie died, she made it clear that she didn't want us to get another animal. I can understand. If we have a pet, it gives all the other tenants the right to have one."

"I don't mean a pet," he said. "I mean a dog guide. A dog like Elsa."

"Elsa's too big for me." I had offered the first objection that came to mind.

"You know that I didn't mean a dog exactly like Elsa." Bill spoke with exaggerated patience, the kind of patience one uses with an especially slow child. "They match the person and the dog."

"I don't know, Bill." I was serious now, and he sensed it.

"Everybody's hesitant about getting the first dog, at least they should be. It's a big step, and you should think about it, but I know you'll say yes."

And as though to add her own special persuasion, Elsa came over and laid her head in my lap.

There are so many myths—and downright exaggerations—about dog guides for the blind that it's no surprise to me that they are frequently misunderstood by the general public, and often by the blind themselves.

For instance, dog guides are thought to be fierce and protective of their blind owners to the point of danger. Nothing could be further from the truth. They are trained as guides, not as guard or attack dogs. Some of them would, if pushed far enough, protect their owners, and others might not, depending on their breed and personality.

Another myth is that you should never pet a dog guide. In a way, this is true. Dog guides should never be touched by anyone except their owner when they are "working" and wearing their harness. Out of harness, though, they are like any other dog, ready and willing to accept love and usually ready to play.

Elsa was no exception. As she stood there with her big head on my lap, it was as though she, too, was urging me to take the step that in many ways would change my life forever. Still, was I ready for that change? The training would be rigorous, requiring the physical stamina to walk sixteen blocks a day. Simply put, it would require a lot of guts.

Suddenly, as I sat there and stroked Elsa's ears, those twenty-six days of training seemed to stretch in front of me like a mountain peak, rough and insurmountable. I couldn't do it. It wouldn't be worth it!

Then the freedom offered at the top of that mountain seemed to beckon to me, a voice calling, almost pleading. It was the voice of my own secret longing.

I suppose all of us who are blind have it in varying degrees, that longing to be free. We yearn to walk along streets and roads with the feeling of confidence that comes only with the certainty that your next step will be a safe one. Of course, we feel that confidence when we are walking with a trusted human guide, but it isn't the same. It is more like the condition of the bird flying in the safety of a large enclosure. He is free, but his limited safety lacks that spark of adventure felt by his fellows who fly high and free. The world is theirs to savor, to explore.

A measure of that freedom was mine when I learned to use my cane, but that spark of total freedom of mobility was still lacking, and I found myself reaching toward that voice on the mountain. Still, I was hesitant. There was much to gain, but I knew there could be much to lose, not the least of which would be my morale if I failed. For me, that fear of failure was an obstacle of huge proportions.

"Think about it," Bill said, and he startled me back to Ed's living room, with its cozy sound of the gas log and the ticking of the mantel clock.

"All right," I promised, not daring to say how much I'd already thought about it.

Chuck and I talked about it that night as we were getting ready for bed.

"But suppose I fail," I said.

"You won't fail." He took my hand. "You won't fail, because you want it so much."

"How do you know how much I want a dog guide?" I asked, smiling. He always knows what means a lot to me, knows and wants it as much as I do. But this was different. He couldn't fool me. Oh, he wanted my independence, for me, but he wanted that dog to love and play with.

"I could see it in your expression when you were talking to Bill. You know I love taking you places, but I know how much your independence means to you. It's part of the reason I love you. You know, too, that if for some reason you fail, I won't care. I want it for you, because I know what it means. Besides, God won't let you fail."

"Do you think we could pray about it?" I asked, somehow feeling like that little girl who had first gone away to school with so much fear and hope.

"You bet we can," he said, and we bowed our heads.

* * *

"Mrs. Campbell, this is Ed Ruche from Guiding Eyes for the Blind. Bill Parker said that you were interested in a dog."

I had finally given in after about a month, and Bill had referred me to Guiding Eyes for the Blind in Yorktown Heights, New York. Now I was already beginning to regret the whole thing. Almost. I wasn't sure I wanted to talk to the man on the phone, to ask him to put me on the waiting list.

I cleared my throat, and took the plunge into what was probably the coldest and most uncertain waters of my whole life. "Yes, I am." Another little clearing gulp. "Very much."

People tend to call all dog guides for the blind Seeing Eye dogs, just as some people still tend to call all facial tissues Kleenex, and for the same reason. Just as Kleenex is probably the oldest tissue company, Seeing Eye in Morristown, New Jersey, is the oldest dog-guide school in the country. However, there are many equally good schools today, and Guiding Eyes for the Blind is one of them.

In June I received a call from Guiding Eyes to say that my application had been accepted and I was enrolled in the class that would begin on August seventh and end on September first. I have never been so happy and so apprehensive, both at the same time, in my life.

As I replaced the receiver, the phone rang again.

"Phyl, this is Ginny."

Ginny was Mrs. Keister's niece. Mrs. Keister, my first housemother at the Virginia School for the Blind, had been in the hospital for almost a week. I could tell by the tone of Ginny's voice that she had bad news.

"Aunt Matt just died."

"I'm sorry for us, but I can't feel sorrow for her." I dabbed at the tears that wouldn't stop.

"She was ready to go," Ginny agreed. "Will you play for the service?"

"Of course," I said.

We talked for a while longer, and as I replaced the receiver, I thought about that selfless woman who had been a mother to countless blind children, instilling a sense of self and independence even in the most awkward and timid. I had always been inspired by her pride in me; so had all her children. She would have been so pleased and proud to hear that I had been accepted by Guiding Eyes. I would succeed. No matter how difficult it was, *I would succeed.*

But as the time drew closer, I began to lose that confidence. It would stay with me during the busy hours of the day, but in the quiet of the night, it would return, seeming almost to suffocate me.

The worst of it was that I felt that I couldn't confess it, not even to Chuck. Everybody was so excited about my going away to get a dog that I couldn't bring myself to admit I thought I might fail. Now, safely insulated from that fear of failure by the passing of years, my silent pride seems foolish, to say the least. At the time, though, it was a huge, dark monster.

Finally, I took courage in hand and confessed my fear to Larry Wilson, who, several months earlier, had replaced Roger Madden as the minister at the little church where I played the piano.

"You know, Phyllis," he said, "you're like the children of Israel in the Bible. They wanted their freedom, worked for it, sacrificed for it, wandered in the wilderness for it. Then, when they were ready to cross the Jordan into the Promised Land, they lost their nerve for a while. They lost sight of the promise, because all they could see was that river. But remember, God showed them where to cross in safety. He'll be with you. I'd be a little worried if you weren't afraid."

Did that reassuring conversation send my fear into limbo? I'm afraid not, but it did give me a new measure of courage, and before I knew it, Chuck was checking me in at the airport in Charlottesville on August seventh.

"Don't worry, sir," the clerk said. "Somebody will be waiting in Washington to help your wife change airlines."

That was the least of my worries at the moment. What was I doing?

"I'll miss you," Chuck whispered as we walked toward the plane. "I got a little something for you. I was afraid you'd get hungry." He put two large bars of milk chocolate in my hand. I recognized them by the crinkly wrapper. They were my very favorite brand, and tears filled my eyes. I don't think I would have cried if it had been some expensive parting gift. My tears were for the thoughtfulness that had made him pick this small treat for me. I would miss him more than I could say, but he would be there with me, safe in my heart.

Two days later, on that hot August morning, I sat on the grass at the school, remembering all that had led up to my being there. Once again, I wondered what on earth had ever made me think I wanted a dog.

They had presented him to me the afternoon before, a black Labrador named Lear. Because I have always loved dogs, I felt a fondness for him, but something was missing. Where was that spark of oneness I had expected to feel with this sixty-four pounds of life that was supposed to act as my eyes?

I sat there and held Lear's leash, waiting for my turn to go for our first walk. How could I explain to everybody that it just hadn't worked? How could I explain my failure to grasp the thing I had talked about, planned for, even prayed for in the deep secret part of me that had longed for the freedom offered by a dog guide?

"Phyllis and Lear."

It was the voice of Dave, the trainer in charge of my class of six. Now it was our turn, Lear's and mine. I got up, giving Lear a pat.

We had been carefully matched, dogs and owners, according to physical traits and personality. The two trainers, Pam and Dave, had observed all the students since our arrival at the school on Saturday, and they had assured me that Lear and I were a perfect match. But as I started toward the sidewalk, I wasn't sure. I wasn't sure of anything, to tell the truth.

"Okay." Dave showed me how to hold the harness handle and leash together in my left hand. "Tell him to go forward the way I explained yesterday."

"Lear, forward," I said, surprised at the assurance in my voice.

And we were off at a brisk pace.

"You just passed a cat," Dave told me, and I heard the pride in his voice. "Lear didn't even look at it, just the way he's been trained."

And then it happened—that spark of love and trust. I had known, of course, that dog guides are trained to ignore everything but the safety of their blind owners, that in a sense they give up most of their doggie lives for their owners. Now, here it was, but with one big difference. This was not just a dog guide. This was Lear—*my* Lear—and he was doing all that not just for his blind owner, he was doing it for *me*. Lear was my dog and I was his. We belonged to each other and to no one else in that particular, special way.

As we turned the corner, the traffic suddenly became the roar of a distant river receding into the remoteness of my past. I had crossed safely over that tide of fear.

Thank you, I said silently. *Thank you, God. I'm free.*

And I was free. Free not only to walk in independence, but also free from that crushing and crippling thing called fear. Truly, I had crossed over Jordan.

17

And Lear Makes Three

He believed that he was born, not for himself, but
for the whole world.

Lucan

The next months were filled with magic. Every day took on new promise and deepened my love and respect for Lear.

I never knew anybody who didn't like him, and most people fell in love with him almost instantly. Like most Labradors, Lear was gentle and affectionate, but that was only a tiny part of his charm.

"Lear's a character," one of the trainers said, and I could hear the affection in her voice.

For the first few days after they gave us our dogs, we weren't allowed to touch any of the other dogs in training. That ensured that our own dog would realize that he or she was ours and ours alone. It was impressed upon us that our dog must not see us petting another dog or catch his scent.

It is very special, that relationship between blind person and dog, forged from so many subtle elements, not the least of which is, to put it simply, "ownership" of each other.

A dog guide's early life must be confusing. First he is taken from his mother and siblings at the school's puppy farm and placed in the home of a 4-H family. There he learns simple obedience and the give-and-take of family life, including other animals. If during this process a dog shows unpleasant traits, such as hostility toward people or other animals, he or she is usually not included in the training program at the school. That program lasts from four to six months and starts when the dog is eight to twelve months old.

So, for the second time in their lives, these loving and loyal creatures leave the place where they have known love and security. This time it is to establish a relationship with the training staff at the dog school. Then, finally, they are placed with their blind owner, which means that they must break the relationship established with their trainers.

I must confess to a feeling almost of jealousy when, during those first days, Lear would strain at his leash and wag madly when he saw Dave or Pam, who had been his friends during his training.

"It's so hard not to stop and pet him," Pam told me one day as she deliberately ignored his wagging. "But right now, at least, he has to understand that you belong to each other."

"I'm not sure he likes me." I tried to make my voice sound light, but it really was a worry. Lear performed perfectly in harness, but I can't say how much I wanted that tail to wag for me.

"Of course he does," Pam said, and I knew that she had seen beneath the words into my fear. "We always tell you not to attribute human emotions to your dog, but I'm going to do something like that. Lear's a young dog, not quite fourteen months old, and you're the third person he has been expected to belong to. He'll come around. He works well with you. In fact, you're a perfect team."

"I know. But, Pam, I want him— Well, I want him to love me."

"He will. Just wait and see."

During those first days, too, those dogs went with us everywhere—and I do mean everywhere—even into the bathroom. Then the trainers told us to attach them to the foot of our bed when we left to take a shower or wash up.

It was on the second day of that phase of the training that it happened. I had left Lear with a pat and the assurance that I'd be back in a few minutes. The warm sting of the shower felt so good that I stayed under it a little longer than usual. As I opened the door, letting out a blast of steam, I heard a *tap, tap.*

"I'm glad you're back," Dorothy, my roommate, said.

"Sorry," I apologized, wondering about that strange tapping. "I didn't mean to keep you waiting, but that water felt so good!"

"Oh, I don't mind," she said. "It's just that Lear's been whimpering. Not a whine, but a little whimper every few minutes."

With a quick surge of joy, I knew what that tapping was. It was Lear's tail, thumping the floor. I, the owner of countless animals, had failed to recognize the thump of a wagging tail!

At last it had started, that belonging, which was to grow and blossom for so many years until we were almost a part of each other.

In many ways, the relationship between dog guide and blind owner is like courtship and marriage. There is the coming together, the careful getting to know each other, and the joy and excitement of early love. Then, gradually, that excitement turns into a comfortable, warm belonging, the certain knowledge of what the other wants, what he is going to do. I know that Lear would have given his life in the performance of his duty, and I feel certain that I would have done the same for him.

"You treat that dog like a person!" another customer at the beauty shop told me one day.

"Why not?" I asked, toweling the last of the raindrops out of his fur. "Lear has put himself between me and a car more than once. So far, I can't say the same for any person I know. A lot of people might do it, of course, if they were asked to, but he has the responsibility every day."

But that conversation took place long after those first weeks of learning, of adjusting, of loving.

We learned how to cross streets and how to make our way safely through pedestrian traffic. Lear lay quietly beside me while I played the piano or organ. After all, they were things he would have to do, and we had to be sure the music wouldn't hurt his ears and cause him to howl in the middle of a church service.

"What will happen if he does howl?" I asked Dave as I took my place at the piano.

"Playing the organ in church is your job," he reminded me—and left the rest unsaid.

"You wouldn't take him away!"

And I realized just how much Lear meant to me, not just as a dog guide, but as Lear, my dog. I knew that if a dog didn't work out in the first days of class, the trainer would try another who might suit the personality or needs of the client more. But not Lear!

"He's not going to howl." Dave gave Lear a pat and me a reassuring hug.

I have been playing for an audience since my first piano recital when I was seven, but never before had I been more afraid than I was on that hot August afternoon as I began to play Chopin's Nocturne in E Flat. With what could almost have been a sigh of contentment, Lear settled down against my foot—and promptly went to sleep. He liked music, and if that's attributing human feelings to an animal, well, there I go doing it again. But I'm convinced that it made Lear contented to hear me play or listen to the stereo.

It was drizzling the day Lear and I went home, but as I stepped off the plane and into Chuck's arms, it was as though the sun shone on the most beautiful day God had ever created.

"Is it all right if I pet him?" Chuck asked, releasing me. Too late, I remembered that the instructors had warned us to be a little careful when we greeted our family or friends, because our dog might somehow feel threatened.

"Maybe you'd better offer him a hand to sniff," I started to say, when Lear took matters into his own paws. Forgetting that he was a proper working dog with grave responsibilities, he rose up on his hind legs, tail wagging, and gave Chuck a wet doggie kiss.

"He acts like he knows me already," Chuck said, hugging him.

"I let him sniff every letter you sent me, and each time I told him that was Chuck. This morning, and all the way home, I told him we were going to see Chuck. I think he knows how special you are to me."

So our life together had started. Now we were the three of us.

If the relationship between dog guide and blind owner is like a good marriage, the introduction of the dog into the family and community is much like the coming of a new baby. Everybody, from the letter carrier on, wants to see him and find out everything about him. This was especially true when I brought Lear home, because at that time he was the only professionally trained dog guide in Staunton. I was asked to speak at clubs and obedience classes, and Lear was showered with little presents.

Of course, our first trip was to visit Ed and Grandma Ayres and Uncle Raymond. Predictably, they all fell in love with Lear, and he scampered around the house as though he belonged there.

A couple of years earlier, Ed had bought a big house at 833 West Beverley Street. He lived upstairs, and Grandma and Uncle Raymond lived downstairs. Lear felt that the whole house belonged to him.

Chuck, Ed, and I were catching up on everything that happened while I had been away, when we heard a commotion downstairs in the hall.

"You're a good dog," Grandma was saying, and I heard the splash of water.

Too late, I realized why Lear had been pacing back and forth. He had been trying to tell us that he needed to go out, and we had ignored him. The accident had been my fault.

Still, I rushed downstairs to give Lear a reprimand and to apologize to Grandma.

"It's all right." I heard Grandma return the mop to its place, then bend to pet Lear. "Lear's a good dog," she added in the same tone she would use with a child.

To tell the truth, I completely forgot about the incident until one rainy day about a week later, when it was brought back dramatically. It was almost a repeat of the previous episode, right down to the little commotion downstairs in the hall, accompanied by the swish of the mop.

"I don't believe it!" I rushed down the steps. "Did he do it again?" I asked as I reached the exact spot of Lear's earlier crime.

"Lear couldn't help it," Grandma was saying. "Lear's a good dog."

And then it all clicked together in my mind. Grandma had given Lear what he had taken to be praise the time before. He thought that it was permissible to use her hall floor for a bathroom. Well, maybe, as with a child, some instinct had warned him that it wasn't really all right, but Lear hated rain and he was taking a chance.

"I'll have to punish him," I said firmly, although I felt a wild impulse to laugh, especially when Grandma fled out of earshot while her "child" received a sound scolding.

When I went to find her and give her a hug, I felt tears on her cheek.

"I did something wrong," she said.

"No, I did. In the first place, I should have been paying more attention to what he was trying to tell me. Second, I should have realized that he thought you were praising him. He knows better now and has probably forgotten about it."

"I guess they're just little kids, and they have to be taught," Grandma said, obviously feeling better. "I know one thing, though. I'll have to be careful what I say to little Lear from now on."

And I heard her push "little" Lear's head off the kitchen counter, where he was exploring a pan of freshly baked corn bread.

Yes, indeed, I thought as I went back upstairs to Ed's apartment. We were all learning. Somehow, I had the feeling that we would learn a lot more before we were through.

It wasn't long before I learned another valuable lesson.

"I'm sorry, Mrs. Campbell," the funeral director said, "but you'll have to put your dog in that little alcove at the side of the organ. We'll be seating the family behind where you're sitting on the organ bench, and I'm afraid somebody will fall over him."

Something warned me that that wouldn't be a good idea. It was barely a month since Lear and I had come home from training, and he wasn't all that sure I wasn't going to give him up to still another person and his lifestyle would change yet again. I knew all this, but I couldn't see the harm. After all, Lear would be just around the corner. So, against my better judgment, I deferred to the director. Everything went fine until after I'd finished the prelude and Mr. Wilson started reading from the Scriptures.

The first sign of trouble was a tiny little whimper. I was accompanying the reading with soft music, and I played a little louder, trying to drown out the sound. Mr. Wilson read a little louder. Lear's whimper became a whine, which finally turned into a howl as Mr. Wilson and I both increased our volume.

"Oh, bless his heart," a woman a couple of rows back said. "He's crying just like he's a person."

With a sigh, I decided that, whether somebody tripped or not, when I reached a place where I wasn't required to play, I'd have to get Lear. That was my second mistake of the day. When Lear saw me, he jumped up and began to wag his tail—*bang, bang!*—against a heat vent. The racket seemed to reverberate all over the church.

I quickly undid his leash, which was fastened around the leg of a pew in the alcove, and fastened him in his usual place next to the organ bench. Maybe I would never, never have to play for another funeral!

Ginny, Mrs. Keister's niece, was a member of the congregation, and she called me later that afternoon to tell me how nice she thought the music had been.

"I'm amazed you could hear anything over the racket Lear made," I said.

"Now, Phyl, it wasn't that bad." I could hear her laughter ready to come rushing out. "Most people didn't even hear him. I bet everybody who did thought it was sweet. He was mourning too."

"No, he wasn't, and it isn't funny."

But by then it was beginning to be, if not funny, less catastrophic. "I just can't understand what on earth caused him to behave that way. I was right there."

"There must have been a reason," she insisted.

About an hour later, just as I was taking a cake out of the oven, the phone rang.

"I found it!" Ginny announced, and there was no mistaking the triumph in her voice. "I went over to the church and got down on the floor at Lear's height. They had moved a pedestal to make room for the casket, and Lear couldn't see you. He thought you'd gone and left him, and he was worried."

"He still didn't have to carry on like that," I said, but I was relieved. I knew what the problem was, and in the future I could find a remedy.

"Next time, make them seat the family on the other side of the church," Ginny suggested. "That way, he can stay where he usually stays. Now, stop fussing about him."

Just then I heard a suspicious noise coming from the kitchen.

"Hang on, Ginny," I said. "I need to see about my cake. I left it on the counter."

"I hope Lear has eaten it all. If he has, it's your fault. You know how he loves pound cake, and you shouldn't tempt him like that."

"He didn't eat it all," I reported when I came back to the telephone. "Only one big piece."

With that, the tension of that long day broke, and I was laughing along with Ginny.

"You're right," I admitted. "I know how much food tempts him, but, like a lot of people, I expect a dog guide to be perfect."

"Are you?"

She had me there. We live in an imperfect world, inhabited by imperfect people and animals. I would just have to be patient. One day that strange combination of perfectly trained working dog and puppy would mature.

I don't remember whose funeral I had been playing for. Probably, it was the relative of a member of our congregation. If I live to be a very old lady, though, I'll never forget that day.

18

The Tapestry of Life

*The hilltop hour would not be half so wonderful if
there were no dark valley to traverse.*

HELEN KELLER

Drops of moisture oozed from the August sky like drops of
reluctant tears, bringing no relief from the drought and heat
that had held the county in their grip all of that seemingly
endless summer. The wind touched the dry branches of the
pines in a sighing accompaniment to my own mood as I
crossed the patio and went inside.

It was 1975, and for me "energy crisis" had become more
than a phrase denoting inconvenience. Two years before we
had moved from our apartment in Staunton and bought a
mobile home so that we could be closer to Chuck's new job.
It had seemed like a dream in a way—our first real home, tiny
and perfect in its ease of care. The nearby woods were filled
with birds whose song brightened my days, and the stealthy
movements of nocturnal animals added a spice of mystery to
the familiar calls of the whippoorwills. The quiet driveways

in the mobile-home park were a perfect place for the walks Lear and I loved, and I usually felt like the Pied Piper with half the children in the park following after us.

There was a local taxi service, and I was delighted to find how inexpensive it was to go into town, where I could visit with Grandma and Uncle Raymond and do my shopping as usual.

Then came the energy crisis, with the price of gasoline skyrocketing and taking taxi fares along with it. The fare into Staunton more than doubled, as did the cost of the fuel oil that heated our once-thrifty home. Abruptly, my excursions into town had to stop except for absolutely necessary shopping.

Of course, Chuck could take me shopping on Saturdays, but it wasn't the same. In horror I saw my cherished independence, won with so much hard work, vanishing.

I felt trapped—trapped by our tiny home, which until recently had seemed like a dollhouse, and trapped by expense and loneliness. Worse, somewhere deep in the hidden part of myself, I felt trapped by my blindness and the loss of what I thought of as my independence.

Listlessly, I gathered the breakfast dishes and carried them to the sink. In his favorite corner of the kitchen, Lear chewed on a ham bone I had given him earlier.

"Dear old boy," I told him, "what would I do without you?"

Chuck's new job was a demanding one. Often it was after eight o'clock before he got home. At times the world would have been a bleak place for me without Lear, who was always there, always ready to do my bidding, never questioning, never complaining.

I rinsed the dishes and left them in the sink. There would be more than enough time to do them later. I made my way along the hall to the little room I used as a study.

On this morning, however, my Braille writer held no invitation for me to work on an article or a story. My talking book did not seem to call me to listen to a recorded book, and I almost prayed that the telephone wouldn't ring. Even the afghan I was knitting held no challenge. I felt sorry for myself. I knew it, and just then, I didn't care. In fact, to be completely honest, I was enjoying my self-pity.

Then, suddenly, I heard a dry, gurgling sound coming from the hall.

"Lear!" I called, only beginning to feel the edge of fear.

Obediently he ran to me, bringing with him that noise like the sound of a straw sucking against the bottom of an empty glass.

"Lear, what's wrong?" I asked, fear raising the pitch of my voice. But even as I asked, I knew. He was choking on a piece of that bone. Why hadn't I checked to find out if he'd managed to chew it to a dangerous size? Why had I ever given it to him?

"Oh, Lear! Spit it out!" I begged uselessly, foolishly. "Oh, please, boy! Get rid of it!"

Lear and I were about evenly matched in weight, each about ninety pounds, but in my terror I managed to turn him upside down, hoping the bone would be dislodged. Nothing happened, and that awful sound of impending death continued.

As I released him, his terror mingled with mine, and he ran from the room, spraying froth against my slippered feet.

I had to have help, but there was no one around. The few neighbors I knew were all working, and Chuck was too far away. My vet? There wasn't time for that, either.

The friend who had been my constant companion, my very eyes, the one who would willingly give his life to save mine, was dying, dying because of my carelessness, and there was nothing I could do.

At least I could be with him. I ran to where he crouched

next to the living room sofa. I touched his once soft coat, now dry and rough from his struggles to breathe. Was this, then, how it was to end, that relationship of trust and love? Was it to end here in this place where we had been so happy? Was it to end in suffering and fear and death, death that could have been prevented?

No, I couldn't let it.

"Please, God, do something," I prayed aloud.

But there is nothing to be done, the dark fear within me replied. I wouldn't listen to it!

"Please, God, show me what to do. You always hear. Please, God!"

And as I crouched there beside Lear, I felt a sense of calm. It was almost as though a reassuring presence had come into the room.

I heard it then, the sound I had been too frightened to notice before, the sound of bone against teeth.

"Lear, open!" I forced his head up and back with the choke collar. Carefully, slowly, I worked my hand into his mouth. With relief, I could feel that the piece of bone wasn't in his throat at all. It was firmly wedged between his jaw and teeth, forcing his tongue down his throat. Lear wasn't choking on the bone. He was strangling on his own tongue.

Thanking the Lord for my training in first aid, I grasped his tongue and firmly pulled it forward, opening the air passage.

I would have to work the bone loose with one hand while I continued to hold his tongue with the other. If I just had somebody to hold him!

"Well, you don't," I told myself, and got to work. I spoke such soothing baby talk that, at any other time, both Lear and I would have been mortified.

Finally, after cutting my hand against Lear's teeth and bruising his tongue, I was able to free the bone. All during the process, Lear hadn't moved a muscle. It was as though he knew what I was trying to do and understood that his part was to do nothing.

For a long time, we just lay there together on the carpet, my arms around Lear and his front paws on my shoulders. Then he proved once again that, in spite of his training and intelligence, he was still a dog. Tentatively, he reached toward the piece of bone still in my hand.

Later that day, I sat and listened to the welcome sound of rain on the metal roof. The bone was safely buried at the bottom of the garbage can, and Lear lay sleeping beside my chair. The damp air blowing through my study window smelled of the pines, and I could imagine their leaves almost reaching to gulp at the long-awaited rain.

I had put a loaf of yeast bread in the oven, and the smell of the bread and the rain reminded me of home, of so many things I had forgotten.

Of course, Lear had given me greater independence, but in the heady joy of physical freedom, I had lost sight of the true meaning of independence, which is a thing of the heart, of the spirit.

Mama and Daddy had given me independence when they gave me the opportunity to go to school. Nez had given me another kind of independence when she guided my fingers over those first Braille letters. Fay and Lively had given me the independence of knowing I was loved. And Chuck, who offered that gift of all gifts, his life as a part of my own, had given me the independence of knowing that, no matter what, he was there, there to love me and to respect my right to be myself.

Independence is a tapestry of interwoven threads, each adding color and texture and strength to the other.

I had been forced to face death on that hot, humid day, and I had been forced to take an unflattering look at myself. I had been ready, almost willing, to give up Lear's life because there was no one to help me. I had even been sure that God could do nothing, while all the time the solution lay literally at my fingertips. I had been so engulfed in fear and self-pity that I had forgotten not only that God could and would help me with the emergency, but that he would also give me strength and courage for the simple everyday problems that often loom much larger than they actually are.

Yet again, I realized how many lessons God teaches us through His creatures, if we will just look for and profit from them. And God isn't through teaching me about independence. He won't be until He launches me on that final learning experience we call death.

Late that year, Grandma's health began to deteriorate.

"I hate to see them go to a nursing home." The sorrow in Ed's voice reflected my own feelings.

"That's a big house," I said. "Couldn't we let them have the back part of the downstairs for a small apartment? Chuck and I could take the rest of the downstairs. That way, I could be there during the day in case they need something. That's the big problem, isn't it?"

I was sincere about the offer, which everyone agreed was a great solution to the problem. Nevertheless, in the back of my mind, the thought echoed: *Now our little house will be gone.*

I wanted to help Ed and Grandma and Uncle Raymond. I actually longed to be back in town. Still, although I never voiced it, there was that nagging feeling that I was giving up something.

Then, one day as the remodeling went ahead, I realized how much the others were giving up. Ed was spending an enormous amount of money to see that we, as well as Grandma and Uncle Raymond, had a convenient, comfortable place to live. Grandma and Uncle Raymond were giving up a lot of room by moving into that efficiency apartment, no matter how nice it was. I felt ashamed. Everybody was compromising, and I was compromising less than anybody. Silently I thanked God for yet another lesson.

It was almost three years before Grandma's health forced her and Uncle Raymond into the nursing home. They were years of fun and love and caring. I profited in many ways from that time, and even now, years later, I am grateful for days spent listening to stories of the past while Grandma moved around her kitchen, making little lunchtime surprises for Uncle Raymond and me.

They loved us all, but as they left to go to the nursing home on that rainy day in 1979, it was Lear that Grandma embraced in a flood of tears. She could cry for him, could say that she was worried that I wouldn't take care of him, and thus release the almost overwhelming fear and sorrow she must have been feeling at leaving home for the last time.

"Now, you take care of little Lear," she told me as the car pulled away from where Lear and I stood on the curb, and her voice sounded almost normal.

Grandma and Uncle Raymond would be all right. They were together. They would be sustained by their love for each other and their deep faith in God.

I wiped away my own tears, and Lear and I went back into the empty house.

19

Christmas Mittens and Silver Bells

A good action is never lost; it is a treasure laid up and guarded for the doer's need.

PEDRO CALDERON

October of 1982 was rich with the rustle of dogwood leaves mingling with the voices of the neighborhood children on their way to or from school. At times, the air was filled with the sound of thousands of birds, singing a finale to the summer and early fall as they departed for their winter feeding ground. It was all the same, the same as it had been a hundred years ago when the old house was still young and untouched by the sorrows and joys of a century of seasons.

Yes, the fall was the same, but it brought no joy.

We were in the midst of the recession of the early 1980s. Chuck had been laid off two years ago, and there was no permanent work to be had in his field.

"Why doesn't he do something else?" we were constantly asked by skeptics who probably thought he wasn't trying.

After a while, I stopped attempting to explain that he had tried, only to be told, "Sorry, but you're overqualified." He applied for almost every job advertised in the newspapers. He haunted the public library to read the ads in the out-of-town papers, but the answer was always the same: "Sorry."

Ed, who worked for the Virginia Department for the Visually Handicapped, had to visit blind clients scattered over several counties, and Chuck drove for him. This brought in some money, but unless one has experienced it, there is no way to explain the worry and uncertainty of not having a full-time job.

Somehow I'd managed to sustain my optimism until that October. Then it hit me, too, that feeling of loneliness, of uselessness.

"We're not exchanging Christmas gifts this year," I told Nez around the middle of the month. I knew she often did her shopping early, because she ordered a lot of her gifts from catalogs. I knew, too, that it would upset her not to be able to send us her usual token of love, and I wanted to get it over with.

"But I can't do that!" I could hear tears in her voice. "I'll have to send you something. I don't care if you can't send me anything. That's not what it's all about."

"I know, but that's just the point. I know I have your love, and I just think it will be better not to exchange gifts. Please try to understand."

Finally she agreed, and I hung up, relieved that the ordeal was over.

A year before, Ed had moved to Waynesboro, which was close enough for visits, and I was grateful that we would be spending Christmas Day together, but it wasn't the same as those happy days when Grandma and Uncle Raymond had been there. I remembered how we would all decorate the tree and sing carols while Lear bounced from one to the other. Then I'd fix a turkey for all of us, and the old house would seem to smile.

Now Grandma and Uncle Raymond were in the nursing home, Ed had his own home, and Lear was growing old. Oh, Lear still bounced, but he did it with less fervor, and I pushed away the heartbreaking thought that nothing is forever.

"You're feeling sorry for yourself again," I warned myself, speaking aloud. There was more to it than that, though. It wasn't just the thought of no Christmas gifts or the fact that I would miss our usual activities. And suddenly I knew what it was.

I was feeling blue, even depressed, because I didn't have anybody I could do something for. I missed the flurry of buying little surprises, of baking, of knitting some little surprise for Chuck.

Knitting! That was it. I had piles of yarn left over from past projects, and it didn't take a lot of yarn to make children's items. Before I could lose my joy, I ran to the telephone and called our minister.

"Cleve, does Mountain Mission School take gifts of knitted things for the children?"

"I don't know," he said, "but I'll give you the address, and you can ask."

I wrote a letter as soon as I hung up, and in two days, the answer came back:

Dear Mrs. Campbell,

We always need things for the children. As you probably know, we take children from broken homes, children who are orphaned, any child who needs a home. We take them from infancy until they finish school. . . .

Mountain Mission School is located in Grundy, an area that, I am told, gets "more than cold" in winter, so I planned my projects with that in mind.

As soon as Chuck read the letter to me, I got out my yarn and he went through it with me, separating the colors and helping me mark them in Braille.

"We can afford any needles you don't have, and it won't cost much to send the package." I heard my own enthusiasm echoed in his voice. "Do you think you can have everything finished by Christmas?"

"Of course I can." Silently I offered up a prayer that I could. I had a challenge, a purpose.

Soon friends found out about my project and began to bring me yarn, either left over from their own work or bought for my project. The garments began to pile up on the shelf that we had cleared for them in the linen cabinet.

There were baby sweaters with caps and bootees to match. There were sweaters for older children. There were hoods and hats. There were mittens and scarves. And there were even two pairs of cable-knit socks for the teenagers. Listening to the talking book or the stereo, I knitted day and night, and I was never happier.

At last, it was all finished. The last item had been packed and the package was on its way. It was the week before Christmas, and I still had to finish the sweater I'd been knitting in secret for Chuck. When he came home the day before, I'd heard a bag rustling, and I knew there would be some tiny surprise for me too. My whole being was filled with a sense of warmth and love.

Now I would have to hurry. I have always made my Christmas cakes well in advance, but that year there hadn't been time. I got to work, chopping nuts, searching for the recipe that I systematically lose every year—and always manage to find just in time.

And as I worked I remembered. . . .

The year in the country that Gray Boy had climbed to the top of the Christmas tree. The year Nez and I had hung the Christmas tree from the ceiling to keep Miss Muffet from knocking it over. The year Uncle Raymond and I had alienated Grandma for several hours by chasing a barking Lear around the house with a frozen turkey, Uncle Raymond gobbling like a turkey. "You're scaring little Lear," Grandma said, and retired to her bedroom for the rest of the afternoon.

None of us had known just how much we had, I thought as I chopped the orange peel, and I made myself a promise to hold the bright jewels of those good times close on the shelf of my memory.

On Christmas Eve they came, the letters from the school. There was a small greeting from almost every child and teacher, and they all spoke of my generosity.

But I wasn't generous. I had given from the loneliness of my heart, had given to fill that empty spot where so many loved ones had lived for so many years: Mama and Daddy, Grandma and Uncle Raymond, Mr. Cronise and Miss Lena, and all the others from the School for the Blind. And Miss Muffet, and Sly, and Bootie, and Buttons, and Mouser—all those people and animals who were no longer with me, except in my heart.

Then, into my kitchen and my thoughts came the sound of the young voices of carolers. The group of children who caroled every year were waiting for us, Lear and me, to come out. I like to think they came to see me, but in truth it was Lear who drew those children to our door.

"Come on, old boy," I said, snapping on his leash. "Your public is waiting."

As we stood together on the steps, it began to snow, soft, gentle flakes touching my hair and Lear's fur like a friendly hand. And as I listened to the familiar words, I realized the truth of my giving. So often we say that we don't give to receive, but that year I had given and received a gift in kind. Welcome though the knitted items were, I finally understood the truth of the gift. To the children, the fact that someone had cared enough to take the time to give a gift of the work of her hands had meant more than the actual gifts. No gift of money would ever mean as much to me as those children's words of thanks. We had all given, and we had received.

"Merry Christmas!" the carolers called as they turned and started down the walk.

Suddenly a little girl ran back to me and took my hand.

"I hope God makes you see," she said. She gave me a hug and Lear a pat. Without another word, she ran to join the others.

How could I tell that loving child that God had given me a gift of sight that Christmas that was more precious than the gift of physical sight?

Chuck was waiting for us when we went back inside. "You looked like a scene from Currier and Ives, with the snow coming down on you and Lear, and the carolers around you." He helped me brush the snow out of Lear's coat. "I wish I could give you a better Christmas."

"There's no way you could," I said. "This one is special in so many ways, ways that I can't possibly put into words."

"I got something for you." He took my hand. "Well, two things, really. One is a little gift, and the other is something I'll give you now. It's on the piano."

It was a tiny silver handbell, which sounded a pure, dainty note when I shook it.

"It's not much," he said, "but the sound is so pretty. I know how you love bells, and I thought it was something you'd like to have, something to keep you company. You, know, Phyl, I'll probably have to go out of town to find a job. You won't be able to come along at first, not until we're sure the job will last."

We both knew how much it would cost to move, especially to take along the piano and the organ.

"I know," I said. I slipped into the circle of his arms. Soon Lear pressed between us, making sure he got his share of love.

Laughing, we reached down to pet him, trying to live for the moment, the night, for each other, for Lear.

Like Grandma and Uncle Raymond, we would be all right. Even if Chuck did have to go out of town, we'd still have each other. We would hold fast to the love that binds us together no matter how far apart we may be physically.

Just before I fell asleep that night, I wondered with a suffocating dread how long there would be the three of us. How long would it be before Lear, too, was a part of memory? Again, as though the act could stop what must come, I pushed the thought aside.

Not yet, please, God, I prayed. *Not yet. . . .*

20

"Good Night, Good Dog..."

Peace and rest at length have come,
All the day's long toil is past;
And each heart is whispering, "Home,
Home at last!"

THOMAS HOOD

I will always think of those first months of 1983 as a special time, a time of peace and preparation.

It was as though, along with the earth, we waited for the spring and the vitality of growing things. At night the traffic along Beverley Street was silent with the quiet that comes only with a heavy snowfall. Sometimes it seemed that we were alone in a world of tranquility known to only a chosen few.

Outside, the silence was broken only by the hiss of snow and that mysterious whispering of a winter night which might be the voices of the trees murmuring in their sleep. Inside, the furnace hummed and popped, and we found ourselves speaking quietly, if at all, somehow afraid of breaking the spell of sweet contentment. For we, like the frozen earth, were waiting.

Then came the days of warm sun and freezing air, and Lear scampered like a puppy, enjoying every second as he nosed the piles of snow, perhaps searching for signs of spring. At last it was April, and the world was alive again. Once more I managed to push aside the fear, the sick, sinking feeling that always came when I remembered Lear's age. It was April, and I was thrown into the excitement of a new job.

I had first played at Bethlehem Lutheran Church the year before, when their organist was on vacation, and when they advertised for a full-time organist, I answered the ad.

"I'll do my best," I told the committee, "but none of your music is in Braille. When I filled in for Mike, Pastor Randy gave me a tape of the service music. I'll do my best to learn the service from that, but I can't promise how well I'll do."

That was the understatement of the year. I firmly expected to fall flat on my musical face, but I needed the job.

"You'll do fine," Donna Frank, who helped with the choir, assured me. I knew that she and everyone else meant it. But I knew, too, that they had no idea what was involved.

The hymns weren't much of a problem, because I could cross-reference them through the tune index in a Braille hymnal from the United Methodist Church. At that time it was the only denominational hymnal that had both music and words in Braille.

My trial service was the Sunday after Easter, and on Easter Monday I started practicing. I put the tape of the service music on the player, placed myself and the machine on the piano bench, and after saying a prayer that was a combination of "Dear Lord, please help me" and "Dear Lord, please forgive me for being so stupid as to think I can do this," I got to work.

I would listen to a phrase, then rewind the machine. Listen again, rewind. I did this over and over until I had the music in my mind. Then I would play along with the tape, singing the words and trying to listen for flaws.

By Thursday I was ready to take myself to the organ, and I was surprised to find that it didn't sound too bad. If people would just sing loud, I'd be all right. Well, almost all right, because I was still afraid that I would play in the wrong place. I had always played for a less formal service, where everything was announced. Now I would be playing a completely different kind of music, with nothing announced. Suppose I forgot where to play? Or suppose I forgot how many verses a hymn had?

I remembered that I had a folder with a clipboard on one side. After knocking half the bookshelf down, I found it. With Chuck's help, I wrote down the order of the service along with the words that would precede the music. Where I needed to play a hymn, I wrote down the name, then the words at the beginning of the last verse. I could put my folder on the bench beside me and drop my hand when necessary to feel the Braille. I was ready!

But by Sunday, I was no longer so confident.

"They'll never take me," I told Chuck on the way home from church.

"You did fine," he insisted. "I felt they were all praying you'd do well, and you did. They liked old Lear too." He patted Lear where he lay on the backseat.

"This is the first time he's ever had his own rug at any church where I've played." I smiled, thinking about the soft rug placed next to the organ just for Lear. "Still, I don't think they'll take me."

But they did, and I was on my way to what is probably the most challenging and rewarding job I'll ever have.

Of course, there was always something new to learn and do, and there were the people. How can I describe those loving, generous people who even thought of a dog's comfort? They included Lear in everything.

Soon after I started to play at the church, Lucille and Gilbert Baker invited us for lunch one Sunday.

"I bought food for Lear too," Lucille said. "May I give it to him, or does he just take food from you?"

I laughed. "Lear takes food where he finds it. It's all right to feed him if he isn't in harness, but you shouldn't have done that. He's fine."

"Well, he was invited to dinner too," Gilbert said.

As I sat at the organ every Sunday, it was as though I had arrived at a little haven of peace and love in our world of change and uncertainty.

In May, Ed, until then a confirmed bachelor, announced that he was going to be married, and our little circle broadened to include Martha.

Martha is one of the most unselfish people I've ever known, yet many people never realize it because she reaches out to others in such a quiet way. It is almost as though she is saying, "I hope you don't mind if I do this for you." Of course, it took a while for me to realize the full extent of her gentle, quiet self, but she won a place of love in my heart at once because of Ed's little cat, Shelly.

Shelly had been a very special part of Ed's life ever since he had moved to Waynesboro, and, of course, after the wedding she went to live in Martha's house with Ed and Martha, and Martha's cat, Bashful.

That was before the coming of the vaccine for feline leukemia, and there was little publicity about the devastating disease that is almost always fatal. At first Ed and Martha didn't know what was wrong with Shelly, who had always been a quiet cat. A visit to the vet revealed that somewhere—we never knew where because she never went outside—she had contracted the dread disease.

Martha loves cats, any old cat, and Shelly was Ed's cat, precious for that if no other reason. Martha worked tirelessly, coaxing Shelly to eat, giving her her medicine. Although she said little, she was almost inconsolable when Shelly finally died. I'm sure she was worried about her own cat, but her thoughts and love were for Ed and his loss.

For some reason, Bashful never got the disease. She is still going strong, the matriarch of the cat population in the Thurston household. Because, of course, Ed and Martha couldn't live with only one cat.

That same summer we moved to an apartment, and Ed put the house on Beverley Street on the market.

"It's as though one part of our life is over and another is waiting to begin," I told Chuck the day after we moved, and I stroked Lear's head where it rested against my knee.

As the summer moved into fall, and the fall into winter, I forced myself to accept the fact that Lear's life would soon come to an end. I'd had him for almost thirteen years, and each day he seemed to be failing a little more. He was arthritic, his heart was bad, and on his hind leg he had an inoperable malignant tumor that grew bigger and bigger.

The holidays came and went, and every night I prayed a prayer so fearful and secret that even Chuck didn't know about it, though I learned later that he had prayed the same thing.

Please, God, let Lear die in his sleep. Please, Lord, don't make me face having to put him to sleep, or to watch him as he dies. . . .

And every morning, Lear struggled to his feet to take me for our daily walk.

* * *

It was February sixth, a day of cool wind and bright sun. The early cardinals and mourning doves sang of spring, and Lear walked with what was almost a jaunty step. He had refused food for two days and had eaten little for weeks before that. The malignancy on his right hind leg had grown alarmingly in the past week, but we hadn't taken him back to the vet. We knew what that visit would mean, and we resisted the finality.

I knew our daily walks must be agony for Lear, and I tried to keep them short. Yet that day, his energy seemed renewed, and he took the lead, ushering me to all our favorite spots on the grounds of the apartment complex, not letting me curtail our stroll. Though I longed to be happy about the spark of life he was showing, something inside me knew the truth. This was good-bye, and I fought against the tears that kept pushing their way to my eyes.

It had snowed two days earlier, and our feet crunched on the lingering snow as we made our way along the familiar walkways that were so filled with memories. Warm summer days when Lear's fur had given off that slightly musky smell of a dog too long in the sun. Fall days when we had paused to sit on a bench and listen to the voices of children from the family unit, and to the sharp whack of a ball as the teenagers worked off suppressed energy after school. And most of all, I was remembering our first snow together. . . .

Cane travel in the snow can be a frightening thing, with all the landmarks covered and sound muffled. With a dog guide, it would be different. At least that's what I told myself the first winter I shared with Lear. But when the first snow came, I wasn't so sure. It began about nine o'clock on the morning before Thanksgiving, and as I listened to the soft ping of the flakes against the windowpane, Larry Wilson, our minister, phoned. When he asked what I was doing that day, I said I was staying home, that I'd decided to postpone a trip to the bank because of the snow.

"You've never gone swinging along all on your own with the flakes blowing against your face, have you, Phyllis?" he asked, and I realized that he had heard the longing in my voice.

"No," I said, and the word came out on a sigh.

"Then it's time you did. Go with Lear. You can do it, and if you feel nervous about coming back up the hill on Market Street, call me. I'll come get you. I don't think you're going to need me, though."

He was right. Lear and I needed only each other that day.

I had never experienced anything like our first walk in the snow. Lear quivered with the pure joy of it, and so did I. The soft flakes kissed us gently, like the notes of a Brahms lullaby as we swung along.

"Where are you going, honey?" Grace, Lively's wife, called from the doorway of the dress shop where she worked. No doubt she thought I'd lost my mind to be out on such a day.

"To the bank!" I called back as we swept by in snowy majesty. "See you later! Give my love to Brother."

Lear was really on a roll. Grace was one of his favorite people, but he was enjoying that snow so much that he didn't even turn his head.

On we went. Every traffic light was our friend that beautiful morning, and soon we were pushing through the door to the Virginia National Bank. Two snow-covered creatures, me laughing and Lear wagging as though someone had just given us a million dollars to deposit.

As usual, Lear headed straight for his favorite teller, Marie Roper.

"I'm coming around," Marie said, and I could hear her making her way along the row of windows and across the carpet to us.

"This is the most beautiful thing I've ever seen!" There was the sound of tears in her deep voice. "May I brush the snow off you both?"

"Please."

By then, those lovely flakes had started to melt, to drip off my knitted cap and down on my nose.

"Everybody who came through that door came through frowning," Marie said, starting to brush me. "Everybody except you and Lear. The two of you came in looking like visitors from the North Pole. I've never seen such a happy expression on anybody's face as the one on yours. And Lear's tail was about to wag off! It brought tears to my eyes to see something that made everybody else so cross give you so much downright fun!"

And the memory brought tears to my eyes now, so many years later, as Lear and I crunched across what I sensed would be our last snow. Where had all the years between flown? I thought of Larry, who had encouraged me to get Lear and then encouraged us to take that first snowy walk. He was gone now, too, dead in a plane crash, one more voice heard only in my heart.

Lear and I moved on from spot to spot, memory to memory. And as we walked, the cold, crisp snow cushioning each step, I talked to him about all the silly little things I remembered about our years together.

"You still sigh if the church service gets too long, don't you, boy?" I said as we turned onto another walkway. "Do you remember the day you went to sleep with your head on the organ pedals, and how I thought there was something wrong with the organ when I turned it on for the closing hymn? It stopped as soon as you got off the low C, but the damage was done. The service was being broadcast that day, remember?"

"And do you remember the day that little kid offered me her ice cream cone in the mall?" he seemed to be saying. "You were not at all happy when I took a lick. She didn't mind, though. Chuck told us that she kept on eating it."

"And what about the time I took your harness off so people could pet you at that kennel-club meeting, and you got in the refreshment line while I was talking? Everybody was disappointed when I heard you and made you come and sit. They wanted to see what you'd do when you got to the front of the line and to the food. . . ."

So many memories, so much love, so much respect. And soon it would end, and Lear would join all the others who moved along the road of my memory.

Suddenly Lear stopped, his nose pointing up.

"What's wrong?" I asked, and I raised my hand. Sure enough, he was pointing to a truck mirror that protruded over the sidewalk. Even now, his training had taken over, and he was warning me about an overhead obstacle.

"You're such a good dog." I bent and gave him a kiss.

What a small compliment to give him, but, as usual, he wagged all over. Nothing seemed to make him happier than those simple words of praise and a simple gesture of love.

We moved off the walk to our usual spot, and I dropped the harness handle so that he could answer the call of nature. The snow had been cleared, and I knew that Jim, one of the maintenance men, had shoveled the path earlier that day. I had made it clear when we moved there that I didn't expect the maintenance men to give us any special treatment. I kept our park area clean, always carrying an extra plastic bag just in case of an unexpected emergency. I didn't expect it, but Jim usually remembered us when the weather was bad.

Now, as I heard his familiar steps coming along the walk, I fastened the twister on my bag and picked up the harness handle.

I felt Lear's head go up, and then a forceful movement from his rear, which told me that he saw his friend. Whenever Jim came to the apartment for some reason, he and Lear greeted each other with great gusto. Now, though, Lear was working, and both he and Jim knew it.

"Oh, my gosh!" Jim called in his usual greeting. "There she is with her dog and her little bag."

"Hi, buddy," I replied as we started toward home.

"See you tomorrow!" he called after us.

"Yes, see you tomorrow." It was hard to get the words past the lump in my throat.

When we got back to the apartment, Lear lay down, and no amount of coaxing could claim his interest. He wouldn't eat, wouldn't touch his water. He just lay there, and my hand on his ribs barely rose as he drew each slow, labored, shallow breath. He had taken me for that last happy walk, and in his own way had shared my memories. He had seen his friend Jim for the last time, and now he was ready. Chuck and I knew that the time had come.

Still, we tried.

"Maybe a piece of his favorite cheese," Chuck said, and he went to get it. "Come on, old boy," he coaxed a moment later.

But Lear turned his head away.

Chuck dropped to his knees beside me, and together we stroked Lear. I could feel his tears falling with mine on Lear's fur. The time had come, and we could only ask God for the strength to bear it.

"Lear knows his work is over," Dr. Wise, our vet, told us a half hour later. "When a working dog is old and sick and can't work anymore, his life is over. You and his work are his reason for living."

"I know," I said. "And I think he wants to go. After his walk this morning, he wouldn't move until we got ready to bring him to you. But he came into your office with that tail waving. Do what we all know is best."

And for the last time, I whispered to Lear, "Good night, good dog."

He had won his rest, had won the right to die as he had lived, with dignity and love.

Later that day I walked along our usual route, only this time I was using my cane. There would be no sitting and feeling sorry for myself, although I didn't know when I'd get another dog. We lived a long way from downtown, and we had no public transportation, but I'd keep up my mobility skills. To do otherwise would be an insult to Lear and all he had given me.

He had devoted his life to me, and had gone proudly and willingly to his death. How selfish I had been to ask God to take him in the night. He had deserved to say good-bye, deserved the right to face death as he had faced life, with dignity and pride.

And as I walked, I found myself wishing that I would be able to live my life in the same way, doing my work to the best of my ability, and accepting the knowledge that it was over with the same grace. Lear had known it was time, had seemed to welcome it.

He had, then, guided me for the last time, not toward some physical destination, but to point me toward the truth about what we humans dread and fear the most—death. It can be a friend, Lear showed me, a welcome release. We should face it with dignity and with hope, for it isn't an ending. It's a beginning.

21

"Just a Little House. . ."

Everyone in his own house, and God in all of them.

CERVANTES

The spring of 1984 was a bleak time for me. It wasn't only that I missed Lear, although that was certainly a part of it, but it was totally lacking in the beauty I had always associated with the season.

For me, for all the blind, beauty is a subtle, fragile concept. It depends on many things not necessary to those who "see" with their physical eyes the beauty that surrounds them.

There is the nesting song of the robin, the wheeling sound of swallows in the sky at the end of the day, the night song of the wind in the leaves, the paean of birds at dawn, the lullaby of rain. So many things make up the beauty of our world.

These are some of the wonders that add spice to my days.

For others, just as for those who can see, beauty may be entirely different. But no matter how we, the blind, "see" beauty, it is as essential to our happiness and peace as the grandeur of snow-topped mountains and the glory of the sunset are to the happiness and peace of the sighted. For me, that spring beauty was completely missing.

Our small apartment was located in a complex that catered to the needs of the elderly and the handicapped. We had been fortunate to get it—I knew that—and when I longed for the songs of birds or the sound of rain through the leaves, I felt guilty and ungrateful.

There were trees and birds, but for convenience and safety, the trees were well away from the buildings. Those who could see were able to enjoy them, and I felt left out when I was unable to answer when someone commented on how beautiful the trees were that spring. I knew I shouldn't wish for what I didn't have, but I still felt sad. Sometimes I longed for the big old house on Beverley Street, with its terraced lawn, roses, and trees.

"Just a little house," I found myself saying in a fragment of a sentence that certainly couldn't be called a prayer. There was no way we could afford a house. I shouldn't even be thinking about such a thing. Maybe I could get some bird records, but that wouldn't do. There would be no sense of the living creatures, no feel of their joy in life and their place in the world.

"This sounds interesting," Chuck said one day in late April, and I heard the rattle of the newspaper. "It's an ad from Hamer Realty. It says they have several fixer-up houses for under twenty thousand dollars."

"They probably don't have a roof," I said, but I was excited, although the modest price sounded far beyond our means.

"We could call," Chuck said. "It would be something to think about even if we can't find anything."

Chuck Hamer's grandfather, Fritz, had established the business, and had been Mr. Cronise's contemporary. Chuck and his wife, Mary, carried on the traditions established in the beginning, and they tried to provide good housing at an affordable price.

"I'll see what we can do," Chuck Hamer told us with enthusiasm when we called. "I warn you, though, the houses in that ad all need a lot of work."

"We don't care," Chuck told him, "just as long as the plumbing, wiring, and roof are in good condition."

So it started. We looked at big houses, little houses, and houses in between. They all had one thing in common—none of them would do.

If we could afford a house, the roof leaked, or it was in imminent danger of collapsing. If it was just what we wanted, there was no way we could afford it, and the owner flatly refused to negotiate.

It was just after Chuck Hamer had called to tell me that the owner of the last house we had looked at had flatly refused our offer that my Chuck came home sounding more enthusiastic than he had for months.

"I saw a house," he called as he came through the door. "It's on Stuart Street, way out almost to Montgomery Avenue."

"Goodness, I didn't know Stuart went out that far." I was trying not to get my hopes up.

"Well, it does. It's a nice little neighborhood. The houses are far apart, and if you want trees and bushes, you've got them. The yard's grown over like Sleeping Beauty's garden, but the flowers are unbelievable. It's sort of like an overgrown rainbow."

"How do you know it's for sale? And how big is it?"

"There's a For Sale sign." He hugged me. "And it looks like it might have about six rooms. It needs work. The gutters are just sort of hanging there, and the porch steps look like they might collapse, but I have a good feeling about it. Since we've been dealing with Chuck Hamer, should we have him find out about it for us?"

"We probably should, but he was leaving for the day when he called before. I don't want to wait. Find the realtor's number. If it sounds good, we'll ask Chuck to look into it for us tomorrow."

"I copied it down." I heard the rattle of one of the tiny scraps of paper, filled with all kinds of information, that usually fill his pockets.

The male voice on the other end of the line sounded skeptical. "I'll be glad to tell you about the property, Mrs. Campbell, but I'm not sure it's what you want. We have a number of really nice houses. Can I describe them to you?"

"This one, please," I said.

We had encountered this before. On hearing my voice, people somehow took for granted that we didn't want something that needed a lot of work. Well, maybe we didn't, but we wanted what we could afford. Given its location, down near the now seldom-used railroad, and Chuck's description of the outside, this house was probably in our price range.

"Let me see." I heard the rustle of paper. "The agent who's listing this property has gone for the day, but I'll tell you what I can. It's six rooms and two pantries. It has a full bath too." That was a relief. Many of the old houses we saw didn't have full baths.

"It doesn't have a furnace."

He sounded apologetic, and my spirits dropped. A number of the places that had looked promising in the beginning had been heated with wood and coal, and there hadn't even been a natural-gas line. I heard another rustle, and my world started moving again.

"It's heated with a gas space heater, just one, I'm afraid. But there is a gas line."

"How many chimneys?" I asked, and again I heard a rustle,

this time accompanied by a clearing of the throat that was almost like a question mark. "What kind of creature is this?" it seemed to ask.

Few people today know the joy of a gas fire, so like a cozy wood fire without the mess. If the heaters are properly installed and maintained, they are infinitely safer. With pleasure, my thoughts went back to the old house on Thornrose Avenue where we had lived for a while after Daddy's retirement. I remembered long hours spent by the "fire" reading, listening to music, or just talking. Few people knew those joys, but I did.

"The description says two chimneys."

Two chimneys! Probably we would be able to have a gas heater in almost every room. I pushed away the thought of how much it would cost.

"What are they asking?"

I had put off the question as long as possible. Then I nearly dropped the phone at his almost apologetic answer.

"Well, they're asking fifteen thousand, but they'll probably be willing to negotiate."

Somehow we'd find the money. Somehow.

Two days later we sat in front of the house, waiting for Chuck Hamer to join us.

"The guttering's in terrible shape," my Chuck said, "and the front steps really are collapsing."

"But can't we fix them?" I asked, beginning to be afraid.

"Sure. The steps, that is. We'll have to get somebody to do the guttering. But if we can get the house at the right price, maybe we can manage it. Surely I'll get a job soon."

Just then we heard a train whistle, and the world began to shake. The realtor had told me that the tracks were right across the street, but I'd had no idea how much noise a train makes close up. I realized that it was one of the few passenger trains still running on that line, because it roared by in what seemed like seconds. I knew a freight train would have taken much longer to pass.

"Are you sure about this house?" Chuck shouted into the silence just as the last car went by. "Sorry," he said, lowering his voice.

"I think it's fantastic," I told him. "Ed will probably want to move in. He's always said he'd like to have his very own railroad."

"I have a feeling we'd soon get used to the trains. Listen. Do you hear anything else?"

"Water! I hear running water."

"That's right. There's a little stream on the railroad side of the street. I just noticed the sound of the water."

I have to admit that just a bit of my enthusiasm deserted me a few minutes later as I made my rather perilous way up the sagging steps between the two Chucks.

Two pushes of the doorbell brought absolutely no response.

"But she knows we're coming," Chuck H. said.

Just then I heard the chain drawn aside on the other side of the door.

"Yes?"

"Mrs. Wright, we've come to see your house," Chuck H. said in his most professional voice.

Oh, no! I thought. *He has the wrong name!* Mrs. Wright had been the owner of the last property we had viewed. The list realtor had told me that the owner of this house, Frances Leach, was an elderly lady who was selling her home and going into senior housing. I braced myself for the confusion and explanations, but I needn't have worried.

"What say?" the woman almost shrieked.

Apparently she was hard of hearing.

"It's Mrs. Leach," I said to Chuck H. in a stage whisper.

"Oh, I'm sorry," Chuck H. said, and tried again.

"Mrs. Leach, these folks have come to see your house."

"What say?"

"These people have come to see your house," he said without raising his gentle voice.

We'll be standing here at sunset, I thought.

"Hello, Mrs. Leach. We've come to see your pretty house," I shouted. "May we come in?"

"Well, surely," she said, and in her voice I heard the ghost of the hostess who had reigned in this place for over forty years.

The house had most likely started its life about a hundred years ago as a farmhouse, and I was surprised at how much it reminded me of Fay and Bill's old house. Downstairs there was a living room, a small dining room, a kitchen, and two walk-in closets that served as pantries, one off the kitchen and the other off the dining room.

"This bathroom is as big as my living room," Chuck H. said as we made our way behind him up the narrow stairs.

That was something of an exaggeration, but it was large, and I'm sure it had started life as a bedroom. I had thought our tub on Beverley Street was the biggest bathtub I'd ever find, but as I stretched to reach from one end of it to the other, I realized this one had it beat by a mile. I couldn't help giggling. It felt so regal, standing there on its claw-shaped feet.

In addition to the bathroom, the upstairs consisted of three bedrooms and a small hall.

There was decidedly nothing grand about any of it, but at that moment, I don't think I would have traded it for the White House. After all, I'd have to leave there in eight years at the most.

"Where's your black dog?" Mrs. Leach asked as I sat with her in the kitchen while the men looked around outside.

"Ma'am?"

"Where's your black dog? I remember him from the senior center. You came to play the piano."

She was right. I had volunteered at the center for several years, and I often did musical programs.

"I didn't recognize you at first," she was going on, "but I remember your dog."

People always remembered Lear. "He died in February," I said.

"I'm sorry." She patted my hand. "I surely am sorry. I've got a cat." I could hear the pride in her voice.

I wondered what would happen to her cat. I had learned from the realtor that she had almost no family, and that her husband had died in the early 1960s. Mrs. Leach had worked at cleaning houses until her sight and general health started to fail. I felt a stab of sadness for her. I knew that most senior housing didn't permit pets, and I realized that the little house, so in need of repairs that she couldn't afford, and her cat were about all she had. Soon they, too, would be gone.

"There's a lot of work to do," Chuck H. said fifteen minutes later as we stood in the driveway, "but this is the best one we've seen. You should be able to get it at the right price. Would you like to make an offer?"

"Do you like it?" my Chuck asked.

"Oh, yes!" I said.

"It's not what you've been used to." I heard the sorrow in his voice. He wanted everything good for me, and I only wanted him. Well, him and a house, too, if I could have it.

"I don't care." I reached for his hand. "I've lived in old houses before—and just listen to those birds!"

"I guess that settles it," he began, just as another train rumbled along. "Let's go draw up the contract," he said in the silence that followed. This time he didn't shout. We were already learning about trains.

22

The Gifts of Love

*I do not fear tomorrow for I have seen yesterday
and I love today.*

WILLIAM ALLEN WHITE

"It's the best I can do," I said.

I turned off the electric typewriter and removed the sheet of paper that would determine whether we could have the little house.

It turned out to be harder than I had imagined to borrow the money. To my surprise, this was less because our income was so pitifully small and more because the house was old and the amount we were borrowing was almost insignificant in the world of loans.

"Why not apply for a low-cost loan on a nice house in the country?" was what we heard most often. At first I tried to explain that I couldn't drive and would be helpless if something happened to my husband. I'd hate being totally dependent on somebody else.

"Oh, people don't mind. Somebody would help you out." Or variations on that theme were my only answer until we applied at Community Federal Savings Bank.

"I can understand your situation," the loan officer said. "Let's see what we can do."

At his request, I compiled a list of our assets, income, and debts for presentation to the loan committee. One minute I'd hope, and the next I'd despair. I had one consolation. Although our resources were almost nonexistent, we didn't have any debts. So maybe, just maybe. . . .

"We've done all we can do," I told Chuck as we left the bank after dropping off our proposal. "Now it's up to the Lord. If it's His will, they'll approve our loan. If He wants us to stay on where we are, we want Him to block it and give us the strength to accept the refusal."

I think that was the hardest prayer I have ever offered. I wanted that rundown little house more than I have ever wanted anything in my life except Chuck's love. But it was a big step, and I knew that without God we 'd never make it.

Finally, two weeks later, the day arrived for the committee to review loans. The day came, and went, and still we didn't hear anything.

"Maybe we'll hear in a letter," Chuck said as he kissed me good-bye that morning. He was driving Ed to Charlottesville. "Try not to worry."

But I knew he was just as anxious as I was. As soon as I knew the bank was open, I went to the telephone. Just for luck, I stood in Lear's favorite place next to the table and dialed.

"Your loan went through just the way you wrote it," the impersonal voice on the other end of the line said. I could hear the woman shuffling papers.

At first I thought I must be hearing things, and then the tears came. To this day I don't know what I said, but I was so full of joy that I could hardly speak. Then the apprehension set in.

Suppose we couldn't make the payments. Suppose there was more wrong with the house than we had already discovered. Suppose, suppose—the list was endless, but now there was no going back. Mrs. Leach had accepted our offer, and the loan had gone through,

Georgia Ellen Williams and her husband, John, had lived across from us on Beverley Street, and I was delighted when I found out that she was rather like a foster daughter to Mrs. Leach. She telephoned me one day just before the closing. "I was wondering if you'd take Mama Frances's little cat," she said.

We had been working on the house so that we could have as much as possible done before we moved in, and we had been feeding the cat, but I didn't even know her name.

"Kitty, kitty, gray cat," I would call when we put out her food. She would come running, hoping, I think, for the one who would never be there again.

I felt sorry for her, but *take* her?

"Oh, Mrs. Williams, I don't know."

I didn't want a cat. I didn't want any animal. No one could take Lear's place, and in my heart of hearts, I knew that I didn't want to make such a commitment. Oh, I told myself that we couldn't afford another animal, that we didn't know when we might have to move out of town, all kinds of excuses. But I knew the truth. I didn't want the emotional responsibility. No, I couldn't take Mrs. Leach's cat, but I heard myself telling Mrs. Williams, "I'll try to find her a home."

Surely somebody would want that cat. But as the time for the closing drew closer and closer, nobody did.

"You'll take good care of my house and Fluffy, too, won't

you?" Mrs. Leach asked that day as we signed the final papers.

"I'll see to it that she gets a good home," I said, not quite telling a lie or the truth. I didn't want a cat!

"I'll take her to the SPCA," Chuck H. offered as we left the lawyer's office.

"No," I said, surprising myself. "I promised Mrs. Leach that her cat would have a good home, and I'll keep my promise. They might not be able to find her a home, and they'd have to put her down."

Although we fed her every day and I talked to her, I had never touched Fluffy until July twenty-fifth, the night before we moved.

"Come here," I said, holding out my hand. If we had to share space, I might as well get to know her. Just until I could find a home for her, of course.

Immediately she came and brushed against my hand. She was purring with enthusiasm.

"Why, she's the size of a kitten!" I said, picking her up.

I held her close and touched her lightly. Her fur was tangled from staying outside, but it was long and silky.

"She's gray and orange and black, all mingled together," Chuck said, coming through the back door. "Isn't she sweet?"

"I suppose so." I put her down.

"It's awful for nobody to want you." I heard real sorrow in his voice.

"All right," I said, smiling. "We'll keep her, but the first time I find her strolling around on the table, out she goes."

"Oh, she wouldn't do that." I heard him bend down and pick her up. "You wouldn't, would you, Fluffy?"

"It doesn't suit," I said.

"What?"

"Her name. She's too regal to be a Fluffy. Let me see. I've got it—Lady Gray. That's it, Lady Gray."

If she minded the change of her name, she never showed

it, and in less than a week, she was answering to Lady Gray as though it had always belonged to her.

Every morning she waited at the back door to be fed, but somehow she seemed to keep her distance from me. It was almost as if she understood that I hadn't really wanted her, maybe still didn't want her.

Did I? I wasn't sure. I was willing to take care of her, but I knew that I wasn't willing to give myself to her.

Then, suddenly, on August twenty-third, the routine of our lives changed.

Chuck got a contract job in Richmond, and although it meant he would have to be gone from Sunday until Friday evening, we were grateful. It had been almost four years since he had been laid off, and we had spent the last of our savings on the down payment for the house.

"I'll be fine," I assured him, although I found myself wishing that I was just a little more familiar with the house and the neighborhood. It was almost exactly a month since we had moved.

"I won't go if you don't want me to," he said.

"Of course you'll go. It will be harder for you than for me. You'll be all by yourself, and I'll be here at home."

"And you'll have Lady," he reminded me. I heard her leap onto his lap.

"And I'll have Lady." I wondered what kind of blessing that would be.

Those first weeks were lonely, and on one occasion downright frightening.

I had gone to bed as usual with a book and had fallen asleep almost at once. According to my Braille watch, it was almost one o'clock in the morning when I heard it. Something or someone was clattering on the back-porch roof. As I lay listening, I remembered that the back-bedroom window opened directly onto the roof. If someone was out there, it would be no trouble at all to break that window, and then he would be in the house.

Hesitantly, I reached toward the telephone. But what if it was an animal? I'd feel like a fool! I drew back my hand. The noise kept up.

What kind of animal would be out there in the middle of the night? On the other hand, what kind of person would be out there making so much noise? Well, that was an easy one. The house had been vacant for almost two months before we arrived. Maybe the intruder thought it still was.

"I'll just change his mind," I said aloud as I grabbed my robe and slippers.

As I went through the house, I turned on every light, including the one on the front porch. Then I turned on the organ, opened the swell pedal to full, and began to play Wagner's "Pilgrims' Chorus."

Either I would scare the person away, or somebody would call the police for me. I'd rather be reprimanded for playing Wagner in the middle of the night than look like a silly idiot who calls the police for no reason.

Nothing happened. No siren screamed into my driveway, and the clattering continued.

"It's either an animal or a maniac who has no intention of coming in," I said aloud after about twenty minutes of Wagner. "I'm going to bed."

But I locked my bedroom door.

"It's a squirrel, a big fat one," Chuck reported late on Saturday when I heard the same clattering.

"But what was he doing up there in the middle of the night?" I asked as I took the rolls out of the oven.

"Who knows? But that's what it is now. I bet the moon was full that night."

He was right. A check of the moon phases on my Braille calendar showed that the moon had indeed been full on that night, and although I didn't hear my intruder for some time, he showed up again almost without fail all that fall on the first night of the full moon.

"Do you want me to come in with you?" Lucille Baker asked one night in October after she and Gilbert brought me home from choir practice.

"Oh, no," I said. "Thank you, but I'm fine."

Although I couldn't see it, I always left a light on to give the impression that somebody was at home, and I felt no apprehension as I flicked the porch light in a good-night salute and heard their car leaving the driveway.

"I'm home, Lady Gray," I called.

This was the first evening I had left her in the house. There was a definite bite in the air, and I'd left her asleep on the chair next to my desk. I often left her in the house during the day when I had to go out, and she always came running at the sound of my voice.

Maybe she was still sound asleep, but a check of the chair showed that she wasn't there.

"Kitty, kitty, gray cat," I called in the words I still used to summon her. There was no answer. She had never failed to come when I called her, and the first stirring of uneasiness moved across my peace.

"Kitty, kitty, gray cat," I called again and again as I went through the house, carefully feeling each chair, each table, each corner.

There was no cat to be found. But I had left her in the house!

Then, where is she? I asked myself.

There was an obvious and frightening answer. Somebody had broken into the house and let her out—let her out or hurt her. But surely not.

A check of the back door and all the windows revealed no

evidence of a forced entry. But suppose somebody had a key?

But who? I asked myself.

Well, how did I know? Maybe somebody Mrs. Leach had trusted, somebody she had given a key in case she got locked out. Maybe she had lost a key tagged with her address. How did I know? I only knew that Lady Gray was gone, and that she always came when I called her.

I searched the house again, and again, even feeling the organ pedals in case she was there. Suppose she was somewhere hurt? What should I do?

"Officer, I think somebody has been in my house because I can't find my cat."

Well, I knew how that would sound.

I'll go through the house one more time, I decided. *If I don't find her, I'll call Lucille and Gilbert. I hate to bring them back all the way from Waynesboro, but they'll understand. They already know how silly I am.*

So, truly feeling silly, but also afraid, I started through the house yet again. Then, just as I went through the bedroom door, I heard it.

"Purr, purr."

"Lady Gray?"

"Purr, purr."

"Where are you?"

I tried to sound loving.

"Purr, purr."

It was coming from the dresser, but I had looked there, all except on top of the small box that held tape-recorder accessories. I had been searching for an adapter earlier that day, and I hadn't put the box back on the closet shelf. Surely she hadn't been there on that small box, which had once held a frothy flower confection known as a spring hat. Surely she hadn't. . . . But apparently she had. Because that was where she was.

"Why didn't you answer me?" I asked, hugging her. I was too glad to find her to be angry.

Then I realized why she hadn't come. Mrs. Leach had told me that she always put her out at night, and I had, too, on the warm nights of late summer and early fall. Lady Gray had been afraid I was going to put her out. True to the habits of her kind, she had sat there watching me search for her. It hadn't taken her long to learn that all she had to do to avoid my notice was to keep quiet, but that friendly purring had given her away. Or maybe she was just tired of hiding. I didn't know, and I didn't care.

"Would you like to stay in with me tonight?" I asked as I put out the lights and started upstairs.

"Meow."

"Does that mean yes?"

"Meow!"

It didn't take long to make what I considered to be a wonderful cat bed with a soft blanket in a big box.

"There!" I said, putting her in and tucking the blanket into a nest.

She purred and settled down, kneading with apparent contentment.

But when I came back from the bathroom fifteen minutes later, the purr sounded different.

"Lady?"

"Purr."

I was right. It *was* different. She wasn't in the box, but cuddled happily on the foot of the bed.

"Oh, all right," I said, settling under the covers.

As I lay listening to her contented purrs, it began to rain. A soft sound almost like a whisper of love.

"Thank you, God," I whispered into the night.

I had so much. I had the little house, which was a sanctuary of my own kind of beauty. I had Chuck's love. And, with surprise, I realized that I had a cat. Slowly, over the weeks, Lady Gray had found her place in my life and in my heart. Without my being aware of it, I had begun to love her.

As I lay there listening to the rain, it was as though they were with me, all those animals who had filled my days with fun and love. I was reminded of that Christmas Eve, the last on Beverley Street. The animals had been in my heart then, too, speaking to me of joy, of sorrow, of caring. I smiled, realizing how foolish I had been even to think of not having another pet.

Of course, there would never be another Lear, just as there would never be another Bootie, or Buttons, or Mouser. But there would always be animal friends for me, each one as special and unique in his or her own way as the others had been. They would always be there, waiting for me, needing me— and lighting my world and heart with love.